Greenhill Books

The
Art of War
in Italy
1494-1529

The
Art of War
in Italy
1494-1529

F.L. TAYLOR, MC, MA

Greenhill Books, London

This edition of *The Art of War in Italy 1494-1529*
first published 1993 by Greenhill Books
Lionel Leventhal Limited, Park House
1 Russell Gardens, London NW11 9NN

British Library Cataloguing in Publication Data
Taylor, Frederick Lewis
Art of War in Italy, 1494-1529. New ed
I. Title
355.020945

ISBN 1-85367-142-8

Library of Congress Cataloging-in-Publication Data
Taylor, F.L. (Frederick Lewis)
The Art of War in Italy, 1494-1529 / by F.L. Taylor
p. cm.
ISBN 1-85367-142-8
1. Military art and science - Italy - History.
2. Italy - History, Military. I. Title.
U43.I8T3 1993   92-41767
3557.033045 - dc20   CIP

Publishing History
The Art of War in Italy 1494-1529 was first published in 1921
(Cambridge University Press) and is reproduced now exactly
as the original edition, complete and unabridged.

Printed and bound in Great Britain at
Bookcraft (Bath) Ltd

NOTE

I WISH to thank Mr C. W. Previté-Orton, M.A., Fellow of St John's College, for much advice and encouragement in the preparation of these pages.

I also wish to place on record my indebtedness to the Acton Library. Owing to the generosity of Viscount Morley this valuable collection of the books of our late Regius Professor is now housed at the University Library, and but for its presence there the greater part of my essay could not have been written at Cambridge.

F. L. T.

September 1920.

Ardet inexcita Ausonia atque immobilis ante;
pars pedes ire parat campis, pars arduus altis
pulverulentus equis furit; omnes arma requirunt.

Aeneid VII. 623–5.

CONTENTS

MAPS

MAP I

Land over 600 metres high

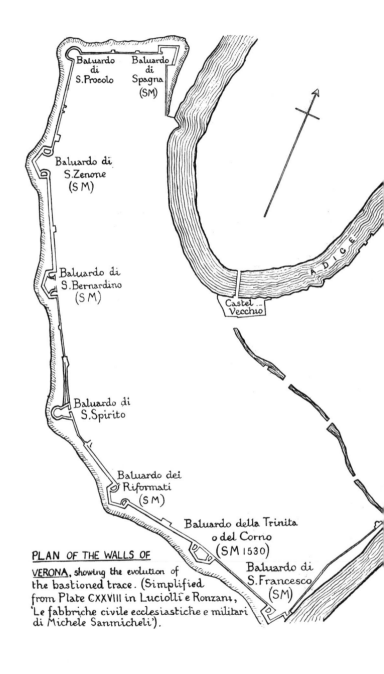

Baluardo di S.Procolo

Baluardo di Spagna (SM)

Baluardo di S.Zenone (S M)

Baluardo di S.Bernardino (S M)

A D I G E

Castel Vecchio

Baluardo di S.Spirito

Baluardo dei Riformati (S M)

Baluardo della Trinità o del Corno (SM 1530)

Baluardo di S.Francesco (SM)

PLAN OF THE WALLS OF VERONA, showing the evolution of the bastioned trace. (Simplified from Plate CXXVIII in Luciolli e Ronzani, 'Le fabbriche civile ecclesiastiche e militari di Michele Sanmicheli').

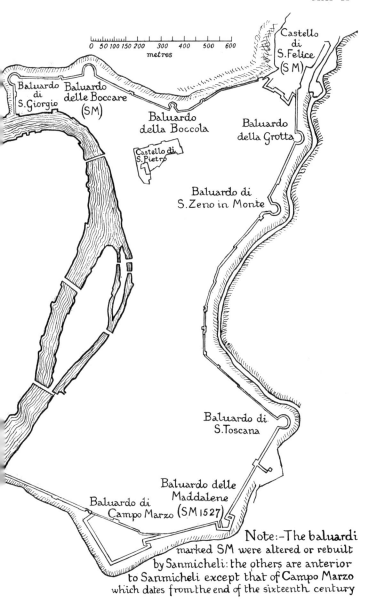

MAP II

0 50 100 150 200   300   400   500   600
metres

Castello
di
S.Felice
(SM)

Baluardo
di
S.Giorgio

Baluardo
delle Boccare
(SM)

Baluardo
della Boccola

Baluardo
della Grotta

Castello di
S.Pietro

Baluardo di
S.Zeno in Monte

Baluardo di
S.Toscana

Baluardo delle
Maddalene
(SM 1527)

Baluardo di
Campo Marzo (SM 1527)

Note:—The baluardi
marked SM were altered or rebuilt
by Sanmicheli: the others are anterior
to Sanmicheli except that of Campo Marzo
which dates from the end of the sixteenth century

MAP III

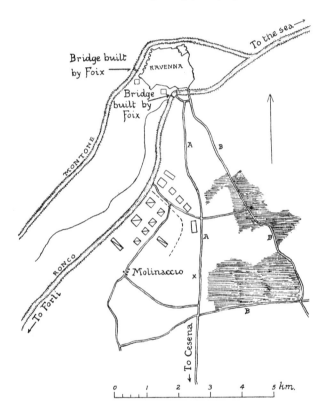

MAP to illustrate the BATTLE OF RAVENNA

French army thus ▢   Army of the Holy League thus ⊠

Trench surrounding the Army of the Holy League thus - - - - -

To the sea

Bridge built
by Foix →   RAVENNA

Bridge
built by
Foix

MONTONE

RONCO

To Forli

A   B

Molinaccio   ×

A   B

B

To Cesena

0   1   2   3   4   5 km.

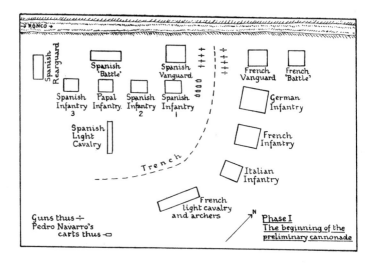

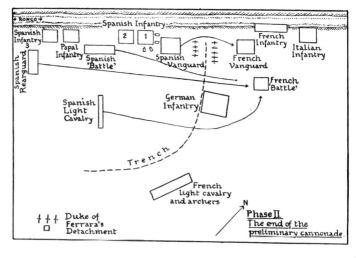

Diagrams representing four phases of the F

MAP IV

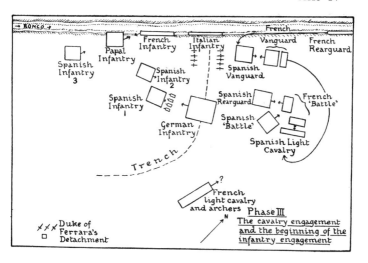

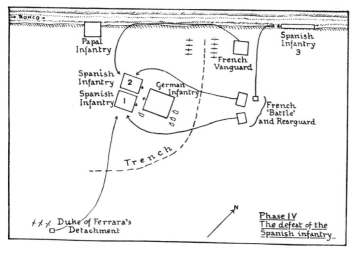

RAVENNA (N.B. Not drawn to scale)

The
Art of War
in Italy
1494–1529

CHAPTER I

INTRODUCTION

THE change from mediaeval to modern methods in the art of war is closely related to the general transformation of European civilization which goes by the name of the Renaissance. The revival of interest in ancient history and literature had a distinct effect on military theory and practice. The new spirit of inquiry and experiment applied itself vigorously to military problems. Moreover the avowed national separatism which replaced the sham imperialism of the Middle Ages accentuated the rivalry between states and produced wars which were more frequent, more prolonged, more general, and more intense than those of the preceding centuries. The history of these wars, waged in an age of eager intellectual activity, reveals, as we should expect it to reveal, rapid progress, amounting almost to revolution, in the use of arms, but what makes an examination of the subject singularly instructive is the fact that the most important of these campaigns were fought in Italy during the culminating years of the Italian Renaissance. The finest minds of the day had the opportunity of witnessing, of recording, and of commenting on the exploits of the leading captains and the most famous troops of Europe. They assisted in the interplay of ideas and the comparison of experiences. The fruit of this period of intensive cultivation of the art of war was the military science of the modern world.

When, in the autumn of 1494, Charles VIII of France set out for the conquest of Naples he did so in a spirit of adventure, at the head of an army raised for the occasion, and with the declared desire to proceed ultimately to the Holy Land[1]. When, in 1529, the treaty of Cambrai brought the Italian wars to a close there had already appeared in Europe such modern phenomena as the principle of the balance of power, trained standing armies, and competitive armaments. In the following chapters an attempt will be made to trace the stages of the process by which this change from mediaeval to modern Europe manifested itself in the development of the art of war. The inquiry will be restricted to the campaigns which were fought in Italy between the years mentioned above, but since during that period Italy was the battlefield of Europe it will be well to begin with a brief consideration of the military condition of the countries which took part in the wars.

During the first half of the fifteenth century France, under the stress of foreign invasion, had evolved the earliest European standing army[2]. The feudal levy had proved unequal to the strain of a prolonged war of liberation and had been replaced

---

[1] Cf. *Lettres de Charles VIII* (ed. Pélicier), nos. DCCXLV and DCCLVIII, and his proclamation on entering Papal territory (in La Pilorgerie, *Campagnes et bulletins de Charles VIII*, p. 101).

[2] Jähns, *Handbuch einer Geschichte des Kriegswesens* (hereafter referred to as *Handbuch*), p. 841.

by permanent organizations of cavalry and infantry commanded by professional soldiers. Cavalry was still reckoned the more important arm and no clear distinction was yet made between heavy and light cavalry. The smallest cavalry unit was a group of six, called a "lance," which consisted of one heavy-armed warrior, or "man-at-arms," and five more lightly armed horsemen—a survival from the days when the feudal knight was accompanied into battle by his armed followers. A true national infantry was raised towards the middle of the century by the en-rolment of a force of *franc archers*. Under Louis XI these were raised to the strength of 16,000[1]. Later, however, they were disbanded by the same monarch, who preferred tò rely on the services of Swiss mer-cenaries. The French infantry which fought in the Italian wars was not national but regional. It con-sisted chiefly of Gascons and Picards and was allotted only a secondary rôle in battle[2]. The main part was played by professional soldiers hired from Switzer-land and Germany.

At the close of the fifteenth century the Swiss were reputed the best infantry in Europe, and their successful war against Charles of Burgundy had

---

[1] La Barre Duparcq, *L'art de la guerre*, vol. II, ch. I, § 3.

[2] Its value was definitely lowered by the incorporation of Swiss and German mercenaries in the French army. Machia-velli, writing from France in the closing years of Louis XII's reign, remarked that the French infantry was low-born and in a position of inferiority to the nobles, and that the Gascons, who were the best of them, were nevertheless cowards in battle (see his *Ritratti delle cose della Francia*, in *Opere*, vol. VI, p. 297).

raised incalculably the prestige of the footsoldier. The contempt in which infantry had been held in the Middle Ages had not been appreciably diminished by the successes of the English bowmen against the mailed chivalry of France, for the secret of these victories had been the keeping of the enemy at a distance: the archer who allowed a mailed knight to reach him was a doomed man. In the Swiss Christendom saw for the first time an army of foot which sought out and defeated in hand-to-hand fight the best cavalry of the day. The weapons and tactics of the Swiss will be considered in detail later: it will suffice to say here that their value was quickly recognized by European sovereigns, and that their high reputation led to the raising of German regiments trained and organized on exactly similar lines[1]. These landsknechts (as they were called), though subjects of the emperor and often enrolled expressly for imperial wars, could nevertheless be hired, with the emperor's sanction, by foreign governments in need of troops. Both Swiss and landsknechts were recruited—in theory at any rate—entirely from free peasants and burghers[2], and both maintained close human relations with their leaders—often indeed influencing military policy by an organized expression of opinion. In these respects they were in marked contrast to the royal troops of neighbouring states. Switzerland did not produce mounted soldiers. On the other hand in Germany as in France heavy cavalry

---

[1] Ricotti, *Storia delle compagnie di ventura*, pt. v, ch. i, § 8.
[2] Rüstow, *Geschichte der Infanterie*, vol. i, bk. iii, p. 203.

remained the most important and the most dreaded arm[1].

Political unity and prolonged war against the infidel had recently produced significant developments in the military organization of Spain. Here for the first time we see the infantry definitely given precedence over other arms[2]. Spain had the good fortune to breed a great soldier, and the Spanish monarchs had the good sense to let him forge the weapon with which he won his victories. Gonsalvo de Cordova, known to his contemporaries as the Great Captain, increased the numbers, reorganized the formations, and revised the equipment of the Spanish infantry, and the result was a blend between the Roman legion and the Swiss battalion of his own day. The Spanish cavalry were reduced in numbers, the light horse were separated from the men-at-arms[3], and both were made auxiliary to the infantry. It was such an army which Gonsalvo later led into Italy.

Among the Italian states in the fifteenth century the art of war made little material progress. The man-at-arms still enjoyed all his mediaeval repute. Footsoldiers were universally despised, no attempt was made to organize them for the shock of battle, and in the tiny armies of the period they were usually outnumbered by the cavalry[4]. The reason for this was partly political and partly economic. Many of

---

[1] Jähns, *Handbuch*, p. 1067.　　　[2] *Ibid.* pp. 1044 *seq.*
[3] *Ibid.* pp. 1067 *seq.*
[4] Ricotti, *Storia delle compagnie di ventura*, pt. v, ch. I, § I; Rüstow, *Geschichte der Infanterie*, vol. I, bk. III, p. 206; Jähns, *Handbuch*, pp. 818 *seq.*

the small states of Italy were governed by tyrants
who were frequently professional soldiers and whose
power depended upon the maintenance of a standing
army. Since the resources of these states were not
equal to supporting a large permanent body of horse
and foot, and since the tyrants were disinclined for
obvious reasons to arm their own subjects, they contented themselves with a few hundred mounted mercenaries, who were both more imposing and more
efficient than the Italian infantry. In the event of a
war between two of the larger states of Italy both
sides would hasten to hire the services of these local
military rulers[1] and of other unattached captains of
mercenaries (condottieri), and the commercial outlook of such combatants would manifest itself in a
long campaign consisting chiefly of manoeuvre and
involving a minimum of bloodshed[2]. Winter operations, work which involved strain, the infliction of
heavy casualties, were avoided by the condottieri[3]
as tending to reduce the common stock of trained
soldiers—the currency on which was based their
political and economic stability. In strange contrast
to this ca' canny practice of the art of war is the

[1] Cf. Machiavelli, *Legazione I*, which deals with the hire of
200 men-at-arms from Jacopo IV d' Appiano, lord of Piom-
bino, by Florence for the Pisan war.

[2] Jähns, *Handbuch*, p. 818. Cf. Machiavelli, *Prince*, ch. XII
and *Discorsi*, bk. II, ch. XVIII; Guicciardini, *Istoria d' Italia*,
bk. XV, p. 73 (Milanese edition, 1803: all subsequent references are to this edition).

[3] Machiavelli, *Prince*, ch. XII. Cf. also Sanuto's phrase concerning the battle of Fornovo, the first battle of the Italian
wars: "non si faceva presoni, come in le guerre de Italia" (*La
spedizione di Carlo VIII*, bk. IV).

kindred phenomenon of the rise of military theory. To the Italian condottieri who fought so sparingly belongs the honour of originating the modern theoretical study of warfare. The intense intellectual life of the Italian Renaissance, combined with the aggregation of a number of competing states within a small area, provided both the atmosphere and the soil for fostering this new branch of human knowledge. The condottieri founded military schools[1] at which they analysed strategical and tactical problems, emphasized the interdependence of the different operations of a campaign, and fortified their arguments with citations from the Greek and Latin classics. It will be readily understood how the new enthusiasm for abstract discussion accentuated the military dilettantism which prevailed in Italy towards the end of the fifteenth century, but this degeneration should not be allowed to obscure the fact that the condottieri were the medium through which the Renaissance, both as a classical and as a scientific movement, influenced the development of the art of war in Europe.

The invention of gunpowder at an uncertain date well back in the Middle Ages had not revolutionized military method. Heavy guns for battering down the walls of fortresses were now in general use, but it had yet to be shown that the mediaeval stronghold was obsolete as a means of defence. Although the casting

---

[1] Ricotti, *Storia delle compagnie di ventura*, vol. III, pt. IV. Such a school is mentioned by Porto, *Lettere Storiche* (ed. Bressan), no. 43, "della quale sono usciti molti dotti capitani."

of lighter guns and the adoption of improved means of transport by the French opened possibilities for an extended use of artillery in battle[1], no clear distinction yet existed between field artillery and siege artillery[2]. The invention of small portable firearms had introduced nothing new into the tactics of the time[3]: they were considered less effective than the cross-bow or arbalest[4], their use was confined chiefly to the less serviceable infantry, and no government attempted either to manufacture them in large quantities or to make their employment the subject of special training. Machiavelli, writing as late as 1520, could still belittle the importance of gunpowder in modern war[5].

To sum up: in 1494 Europe as a whole still regarded the elaborately equipped mounted warrior, the descendant of the mailed knight of the Middle Ages, as the most important instrument of battle. It is true that the Swiss infantry had recently won some astonishing victories over heavy cavalry, and that in Spain the operations of the mounted troops were subordinated to those of the footsoldier; but the Swiss and the Spaniards were not typical of European infantry. Indeed there did not exist a European *type* of infantry. The Swiss and the Spaniards were but two among many local types. On the other hand the

---

[1] La Barre Duparcq, *L'art de la guerre*, vol. II, ch. I, § 5.
[2] Jähns, *Handbuch*, pp. 786 *seq.*
[3] La Barre Duparcq, vol. II, p. 48.
[4] Rüstow, *Geschichte der Infanterie*, vol. I, bk. III, pp. 222–3, 260.
[5] *Arte della guerra*, bk. III.

strongly marked resemblances between the men-at-arms of different countries gave to the heavy cavalry the character and the prestige of an international institution[1]. Gunpowder had been in use for two centuries, and cannon and small arms were familiar objects in all armies, yet there was little sign of the revolutionary changes in siegecraft, fortification, and tactics which we associate with that discovery. Finally in Italy the influence of the Renaissance and the presence of numerous professional soldiers had combined to give birth to the theoretic study of the art of war. Italians were then the teachers of mankind, and warfare was one of the many subjects which they expounded to the advantage of the world. Italy resembled a vast military academy. The comparatively bloodless little campaigns of the condottieri may be regarded as practical demonstrations by professors of the art of war—a kind of giant Kriegsspiel—and the national armies which invaded Italy as pupils who came to improve their knowledge of soldiering. Many of the academic theories broke down in practice—as academic theories have a habit of breaking down—and much of what the pupils learned they learned from their own experiences and from each other. Nevertheless the rapidity of the progress made and the sureness of the conclusions reached were undoubtedly due to the prevailing Italian atmosphere of research, experiment, and speculation.

[1] Jähns, *Handbuch*, p. 1052; Rüstow, *Geschichte der Infanterie*, vol. II, bk. III. p. 197.

CHAPTER II

STRATEGY

STRATEGY may be defined as a manoeuvring before battle in order that your enemy may be found at a disadvantage when battle is joined. It is thus a means to an end. The ultimate object of every commander is to defeat his enemy in the field, but his ability to attain that object depends at least as much on the movements which precede battle as on tactical efficiency when battle is joined. Indeed in modern war the scene and the hour of the deciding action have often to be created by prolonged and painful effort, and it is sometimes the duty of a commander deliberately to postpone a decision until the situation become more favourable to his own chances of success. According to a master of contemporary warfare, it is this preliminary strategic manoeuvring which calls forth the highest qualities of generalship. For commanders directing the strategy of a campaign he desiderates "an omnipresent sense of a great strategic objective and a power of patiently biding their time," and further, "that highest of military gifts—the power of renunciation, of 'cutting losses,' of sacrificing the less essential for the more[1]." This strategic sense, this capacity to envisage manoeuvre and battle as equally vital parts of a comprehensive plan of campaign, was naturally less developed when war was

[1] Viscount French, *1914*, ch. x.

more barbaric. In the Middle Ages, for instance, strategy existed only in a very rudimentary form[1]. The commander of an army in the field regarded it as his primary duty to seek out the hostile force and to offer battle without delay. Elaborate preliminary manoeuvre was discountenanced both by the chivalric spirit of the age, which deprecated cunning in war, and by the desire of all feudal armies to return home as quickly as possible. When, however, professional soldiering began to replace feudal service, and when men began to take more interest in the wars of the ancient world than in the knightly ideals of their immediate past, neither the opportunity nor the means was lacking for a deeper study of the problems of strategy.

We have seen that this study first flourished among the Italian condottieri. By the end of the fifteenth century manoeuvre had acquired such importance in their eyes that it was practised almost as an end in itself. Gian Paolo Vitelli and Prospero Colonna, two of the most famous of the condottieri of the period we are examining, were noted for their opinion that wars are won rather by industry and cunning than by the actual clash of arms[2]. Their campaigns might be described with much justice as a painstaking avoidance of battle. In high contrast to this form of warfare are the methods of the invaders of Italy. The French especially are remarkable for their neglect of

[1] Cf. Oman, *Art of War in the Middle Ages*, bk. v, ch. II and *passim*.

[2] Cf. Guicciardini, *Istoria d' Italia*, bk. IV, pp. 196 *seq*. bk. xv, pp. 73 *seq*.

strategical principles, for their desire to close quickly with the enemy, and for the risks they run in the pursuit of that object. Each of these schools of strategy was tried and found wanting in the Italian wars, but each nevertheless made an important contribution towards the development of a more efficient strategical method. This new strategy is discernible in the Neapolitan campaigns of Gonsalvo, and its use by the imperialists is the determining cause of the final expulsion of the French from the peninsula. Its nature is illustrated by Francesco Guicciardini[1] when he says that good soldiers are willing to retire repeatedly and to suffer delays in their pursuit of final victory, and by the biographer of Giovanni de' Medici[2] when he says that the armies of his day avoided each other till one of them had an advantage sufficient to make victory probable. In other words, manoeuvre was no longer despised, as it had been by mediaeval soldiers, nor was it made an end in itself, after the manner of the condottieri. It was essential in so far as it helped towards the attainment of the "great strategic objective"—the delivery of a final shattering blow at the enemy. The recognition of this truth marks the beginning of modern strategy.

From the strategic point of view the Italian wars which were brought to an end in 1529 fall into four groups[3]. There is first of all the French bid for

---

[1] Cf. Guicciardini, *Istoria d' Italia*, bk. x, p. 285.

[2] Rossi, *Vita di Giovanni de' Medici*, p. 242.

[3] For the geographical side of what follows see Map I.

Naples, which is opposed by Spain and which results
in the subjugation of the Neapolitan kingdom by the
Spanish monarchy in 1503. The second series of wars
begins with the French conquest of the Duchy of
Milan in 1499, is continued ten years later by a
coalition against Venice which pushes French influence still further eastward, and is brought to a
close in 1512 by the expulsion of the French from
Italy. Then follow five efforts on the part of France
to regain a footing in northern Italy: one of these
efforts achieves a temporary success by Francis I's
victory at Marignano in 1515, but the decisive defeat
of the same monarch at Pavia in 1525 marks the final
frustration of French ambitions beyond the Alps.
As a pendant to these three groups of campaigns
there is an unsuccessful invasion of Naples by the
French in 1527, followed by an equally unsuccessful
invasion of Lombardy in 1528.

Charles VIII's conquest of Naples in 1495 was a
triumph of the mediaeval method of direct attack
over the fashionable Italian method of manoeuvre
and delay. Ferdinand, king of Naples[1], refused to
fight in the field and preferred to distribute his army
among a number of fortresses, in the hope that their
resistance would give time for political forces to come
into play on his side. But the new French siege
artillery mastered the Italian fortresses with surprising swiftness, and within a few weeks Ferdinand
was an exile from his kingdom. Strategically, however, Charles's position in Naples was very vulnerable.

[1] He was heir apparent at the opening of the campaign.

The presence of hostile states in northern Italy was
a constant threat to his communications both by
land and sea, and though the cutting of an enemy's
communications did not at that period produce the
immediate decision which it does to-day (since a
large proportion of the ammunition and food supply
was purchased locally)[1], nevertheless an army bar-
ring the path back to France and a fleet commanding
the Tyrrhene Sea could between them have subdued
the French army by slow strangulation. The rulers
of Milan and Venice, who headed the combination
against Charles, were in a position to take both these
measures: yet they restricted their maritime activities to the support of Neapolitan rebels, and gave the
command of their army to a soldier who did not
understand how to make use of a natural obstacle.
The battle of Fornovo, by which Charles forced his
way past the enemy who stood in his path, was not
an indecisive action but a definite victory for France.
It enabled Charles to gain his strategic objective—
junction with his base at Asti—and by that success
to wreck the plans of his enemies. The marquis of
Mantua, who was responsible for the operations of
the Italian army, could have stopped the French
dead by holding the defiles of the Apennines[2]. Instead, he allowed them to debouch into the plain, and
to rest after their difficult passage of the mountains,
before he delivered his elaborate but ineffective

---

[1] Cf. *Charles VIII, Lettres*, DCCCXXI and DCCCLXVII;
Guicciardini, *Istoria d' Italia*, bk. xv, p. 125.

[2] Commines, *Mémoires*, bk. viii, ch. v.

attack[1]. It is interesting to note that one of his motives for delaying the attack was a chivalrous sympathy for a foe in difficulties. In this first campaign of the Italian wars we are certainly a long way from modern strategy.

Guicciardini says very justly that the lesson of Charles VIII's expedition was that the commander who could not resist in the open field had no hope of defending himself at all[2]. This moral was not drawn by those whom it touched most closely. When in 1501 the French and the Spanish made their combined attack on Naples we find King Federigo repeating the mistakes of his predecessor, using his army to garrison fortresses, and consequently losing his kingdom to the guns of the enemy. Very different is the strategy by which in the following years Gonsalvo de Cordova destroyed the French armies and added the kingdom of Naples to the crown of Spain. At the opening of the struggle with the French Gonsalvo was inferior to the enemy in men, in money, in food supplies, and in munitions[3]. He therefore retired to the seaport of Barletta, which he protected on the land-side by strong field defences, and whence by sea he could communicate with Spain, with Sicily, and with his Venetian allies. His sole object in retiring to Barletta was to wait until his army was sufficiently reinforced and re-equipped to enable him to take the offensive[4]. Though biding his time he was

---

[1] Delavigne, *Voyage de Naples*, p. 158 (Godefroy's edition, Paris, 1684); Commines, *loc. cit.*
[2] *Istoria d' Italia*, bk. xv, pp. 73 *seq.*   [3] *Ibid.* bk. v.
[4] Giovio, *Vita Consalvi Cordubae*, bk. II.

never passive. He maintained the moral of his troops by frequent sorties; by personal effort he borrowed money for clothing and paying them[1]; fresh drafts were raised from Germany and the Papal states by the vigorous recruiting of his emissaries[2]. He refused to listen to a well-founded rumour that the French and the Spanish kings had concluded a truce, and when his reinforcements at last arrived he issued from his fortifications, defeated the enemy at Cerignola, and became in a few weeks master of the kingdom.

Later in the same year, by the arrival from France of a fresh army of invasion, Gonsalvo found himself again outnumbered and reduced to the defensive. He barred the road to Naples by holding the obstacle of the river Garigliano[3]. Reacting fiercely to the French effort to cross, he succeeded in confining them to a small bridgehead. The approach of winter induced the French first to suspend operations, and then to distribute the greater part of their army far from the river. Gonsalvo likewise withdrew most of his men to more comfortable quarters, but the arrival of reinforcements decided him to take the offensive at once and in spite of the season. Simultaneously with an attack on the bridgehead the river was bridged and crossed four miles further upstream, and

[1] Giovio, *Vita Consalvi Cordubae*, bk. II.

[2] Giustinian, *Dispacci* (ed. Villari), nos. 434–5.

[3] For these operations see Guicciardini, *Istoria d' Italia*, bk. VI; Giovio, *Vita Consalvi Cordubae*, bk. III; the letter from Prospero Colonna 30 Dec. 1503, quoted in the appendix to vol. II of Villari's edition of Giustinian's *Dispacci*; Machiavelli, *Legazione XIII*, doc. 84.

the position of the French outflanked before they
could assemble their scattered forces. The hasty
withdrawal of the French was turned into a rout by
an unsparing pursuit, and an immediate blow at their
maritime base at Gaeta won the war for Spain.

These two campaigns of the Great Captain bear
the stamp of sound modern strategy. He does not
hesitate to retire if necessary, to refuse battle, and
to act for long periods on the defensive: but all this
preliminary manoeuvre has but one object—the preparation of a final crushing blow. He does not try,
like the condottieri, to win campaigns by manoeuvre
alone; nor is he animated by the rash crusading spirit
which will accept battle on the enemy's terms. He
borrows what is worth borrowing from each of these
strategic schools, and blends them into a business-
like and uniformly successful military method. His
campaigns have a unity of purpose, a machine-like
progression, a careful fitting of means to ends, which
raise him to a high place among military commanders, and to a unique place among the commanders of his own time. His care for his men, the
attention he paid to the interior economy of his army,
and his practice of making thorough reconnaissances
of the theatre of operations[1] also show him to be a
pioneer in the development of modern scientific warfare.

The only strategical point to notice about the
conquest of Milan by the forces of Louis XII is that

[1] Giovio brings out all these points in his *Vita Consalvi
Cordubae.*

the invasion was facilitated by the possession of the "bridgehead" of Asti beyond the obstacle of the Alps. It is doubtful, however, whether the duke of Milan would have profited by the use of the Alps, since he made no attempt to hold the line of the Adda against the Venetians who invaded his duchy simultaneously with the French. This same failure to recognize the strategic value of natural obstacles is shown at the opening of Louis XII's campaign against Venice in 1509. From a dominating position overlooking the Adda the Venetian commander, the count of Pitigliano, calmly watched the French cross into the country which it was his duty to defend. One does not know whether to marvel more at the mediaeval audacity of Louis in crossing a river in the face of a strongly posted foe, or at the doctrinaire indecision of Pitigliano, a true exponent of the methods of the condottieri, who could not bring himself to risk a resolute blow even though it promised certain victory. The blunder was censured at the time. Bartolommeo d' Alviano, the second-in-command of the Venetian army, who had fought under the Great Captain at the Garigliano, strongly urged an attack on the royal army while it was engaged in crossing the river[1], and Gian Giacopo Trivulzio, a condottiere in the service of the French, declared that by allowing the invader to enter their country unmolested the Venetians had lost the war. Trivulzio was right. Vigorous diversions against neighbouring towns forced the Venetians from their

[1] Porto, *Lettere Storiche*, no. 12.

position, and a determined attack on their rear at Agnadello showed them to be infected with the pusillanimous spirit of their leader. Abandoning the countryside to the enemy, they scattered and took refuge in fortified towns. Once again Italian caution had been unable to withstand the uncalculating impetuosity of the barbarian.

The lesson of Agnadello was not wholly thrown away on the Venetians. In the following winter we find two indications that they were beginning to learn the importance of strategic obstacles. In the first place a carefully drawn outpost line was formed for the purpose of guarding the sadly restricted dominions of the Republic. A captain of light cavalry, who was in the Venetian service at the time, has left us an interesting description of this protective scheme[1]. The main concentration of Venetian troops, in the neighbourhood of Cologna, Mantagnana, and Lonigo, was screened by a permanent outpost line stretching along the Tramenga canal and the river Adige and based upon the fortified towns of Vicenza, Soave, and Legnago. The line was strengthened by trenches and strong points, and was held by a mixed force of infantry and light cavalry. In front of this system there were sentry groups, while on the high ground towards Soave was stationed a permanent local reserve. The forward troops were to give the alarm by means of smoke in the daytime and fire at night, and the warning was to be passed back to the rear by the discharge of big guns.

[1] Porto, *loc. cit.* no. 41.

This scheme[1], which appears to observe all the modern canons for the continued defence of an obstacle, was unfortunately never properly tested in practice. When in the following year Chaumont moved forward against the outpost line the main Venetian army withdrew further to the rear and left the garrisons of Vicenza and Legnago to bear the brunt of the attack[2]. Nevertheless the very fact that these fortified towns were parts of a larger defensive system—in other words, that fortresses were subordinated to strategy and not strategy to fortresses—marks a distinct advance in the warfare of the period.

The successful defence of the mountain frontier of Venice against the emperor Maximilian in this same winter of 1509–10 provides the second proof that the Venetian commanders were learning to shape their strategical theory in the mould of topographical actuality. In the previous campaign they had allowed Maximilian to descend from the mountains and to besiege Padua. Now, on receiving news of his approach, they seized the pass of La Scala and the towns of Cocolo and Basciano and thus turned back the imperial army by the action of numerically inferior forces[3].

The coalition against Venice was soon transformed

---

[1] These defensive lines are also described by Mocenico, *La guerra di Cambrai*, bk. II, who says: "si fortificarono con argine e fosse, havendo riguardo a i colli o faciendo ove era bisogno bastioni, accioche pochi soldati difendessero il luogo," which shows that the nature of the problem was fully understood.

[2] Guicciardini, *Istoria d' Italia*, bk. IX.   [3] *Ibid.* bk. VIII.

into a coalition against the French power in Lombardy. The Swiss threatened the Milanese from the
north, Venice remained hostile but cautious on the
east, while the main effort of the coalition, the
armies of the Pope and of Spain, concentrated in
Romagna. Such was the strategic situation when at
the close of the year 1511 the command of the French
army was entrusted to Gaston de Foix. It was a
situation which demanded a swift and energetic
offensive against the main forces of the enemy: such
an offensive, if successful, would effectively scotch
the menace from other quarters. Foix's military
greatness consists in his clear discernment of the
problem and in the admirable rapidity and boldness
of the measures which he took to solve it. The roads
were in the grip of winter: he nevertheless inspired
his men to undertake marches of incredible speed.
The Venetians threatened his river communications
between Romagna and Lombardy; undeterred he
sought the position of his principal foe knowing that
swift victory there would neutralize all lesser dangers.
The Papal and Spanish forces played for time and
refused to accept battle; he drew them after him by
a diversion against Ravenna, then turned and attacked them in their entrenched camp, and gained
one of the famous victories of history. Had he lived he
would within a few days have been watering his horses
on the banks of the Tiber[1]. His death prevented the

---

[1] His orders from Louis XII were to march on Rome
(Guicciardini, *Istoria d' Italia*, bk. x, and cf. the speech before
action which this historian puts into Foix's mouth).

exploitation of the victory and before the end of the year an inroad of the Swiss had driven the French beyond the Alps. It should be remarked that the strategic situation which Gaston de Foix handled so brilliantly was one which demanded vigorous offensive action. It was therefore of a kind which suited both his own character and the tradition of the troops he commanded. In view of the subsequent operations of the French in Italy it may reasonably be doubted whether the army of Foix would have been equal to a campaign which required patience and the postponement of the deciding battle.

The remaining campaigns of the Italian wars are conditioned by the desire of the French monarchy to regain the duchy of Milan, and by the determination of Spain and the Empire (which soon became dynastically one power) to prevent this at all costs. Since France no longer retained a footing at Asti or at any other point in northern Italy, it behoved the Swiss, on whom the defence of the Milanese at first devolved, to keep watch on the passes of the Alps. This they failed to do on the occasion of the French descent in 1513, but the mistake was cancelled by the victory of Novara. At the next invasion in 1515 both sides reached a higher level of strategy. When the Swiss heard of Francis I's preparations they stationed troops at Susa, Saluzzo, and Pignerolo[1], and kept strict watch on all the Alpine passes of recognized military value. Francis spread his army in front of

[1] Barrillon, *Journal*, ch. I.

these on the French side of the mountains[1] and published his intention of crossing by the Mont Genèvre[2].
Meanwhile he caused an unused passage to the south[3]
to be reconnoitred and cleared, thrust a large detachment of his army through it, and successfully
outflanked the position of the Swiss. As a result of
this stratagem and of the victory of Marignano which
followed it, the French remained for six years in
possession of Milan. Curiously enough it was the
passage of an obstacle by a similar stratagem which
led to their second expulsion in 1521. This time the
invading army, under Prospero Colonna, advanced
from the east. Lautrec, the French commander, held
the line of the Adda. Simultaneously with a demonstration of crossing in the teeth of the French resistance a small force was ferried over on the
enemy's flank and a bridgehead secured[4]. Lautrec
counter-attacked too late, and the Adda line was
lost.

During the next three years the imperial arms
crushed three French attempts to regain Milan.
Whereas the methods of the French show no superiority to those which twenty years before cost them the
kingdom of Naples, the strategy of the imperialists
improves with each campaign, and in its final form
closely resembles that of the Great Captain. This

[1] Giovio, *Istorie del suo tempo*, bk. xv (Domenichi's Italian
translation, Venice, 1581: all subsequent references are to this
edition).
[2] Marillac, *Vie du connétable de Bourbon*, p. 155 (in the
Panthéon Littéraire).
[3] The Col de l'Argentière.   [4] At Vauri or Vaprio.

improvement was due chiefly to the influence of
Fernando Francesco Davalos, marquis of Pescara.
Under the guidance of this remarkable man the
manoeuvring of the imperialists developed into a
scientific quest for an opportunity to destroy the
enemy. Unlike the French, they refused to fight
when the odds were against them, but not even Gonsalvo struck harder or with more effect than Pescara
when he judged the time ripe for a decision. The
primary cause of the failure of the French in
Italy was thus the superior strategy of their opponents.

The campaign of 1522, when Lautrec took the field
to recover the duchy which he had lost the year before, was conducted by the imperial commander,
Prospero Colonna, according to the traditional dila-
tory method of which he was a master. His policy
was to occupy strong positions and to refuse to fight.
Had Lautrec been well supplied from beyond the
Alps a decision might have been put off indefinitely,
but lack of money, which produced a mutinous spirit
among his Swiss mercenaries[1], forced him in despair
to assault the fortified camp of the imperialists at
Bicocca. He was repulsed with heavy loss, the Swiss
dispersed to their homes, and the remainder of the
army withdrew beyond the Adda. The following year
Bonnivet, admiral of France, descended from the
Alps at the head of a fresh army of invasion. Colonna
was taken by surprise. He had neglected to block the
passes of the Alps, and the dryness of the season made

[1] Guicciardini, *Istoria d' Italia*, bk. XIV.

the Ticino useless as a military barrier[1]. If Bonnivet
had marched straight on Milan it would have fallen[2],
but the French impetuosity was lacking on an occasion when it would have been supremely useful. He
delayed sufficiently to enable Milan to be put in a
state of defence against him, and then encamped in
its neighbourhood with the intention of reducing it
by hunger. In the winter which followed, no operation of importance was undertaken by either side,
but the death of Colonna, which left the imperial
fortunes in the hands of the marquis of Pescara[3],
speedily changed the character of the campaign.
Reinforced with German infantry the imperialists
issued from Milan, joined forces with the Venetian
army, and then, instead of marching against Bonnivet's strongly entrenched position[4], crossed the
Ticino and attacked his lines of communication. By
this move the initiative was wrested from the French.
Bonnivet followed in haste and offered battle. Re-
fusing to fight on the enemy's terms the imperialists
proceeded systematically to occupy those towns
which served as sources or as channels of French
supply[5]. With his army straitened for food and
diminished by desertion Bonnivet was at last forced
to retreat. It was now that the imperialists closed on
their prey. While the French were engaged in crossing

---

[1] Du Bellay, *Mémoires*, bk. II, p. 286 (in the edition published by the Société de l'histoire de France); Specianus, *De
bello gallico*, bk. I.

[2] This is Du Bellay's opinion, *loc. cit.*

[3] Giovio, *Vita Marchionis Piscariae*, bk. III.

[4] At Abbiategrasso.   [5] *E.g.*, Garlasco, Sartirano, Vercelli.

the river Sesia, the marquis of Pescara struck, and in a two days battle utterly routed the demoralized enemy[1].

The imperial army now invaded the south of France, but was quickly recalled to Italy by the sudden descent into the Lombard plain of a new French army led by the king in person. Of the two armies which now faced one another in the Milanese that of Francis I was superior in numbers, in vigour, and in moral. All these advantages the king threw away. He allowed the enemy to refuse battle[2] and subjected his own men to the rigours of a winter siege. While the troops of the emperor recuperated and refitted at Lodi, the French shivered in the trenches before Pavia. He even co-operated with the season in reducing the effectiveness of his forces by sending a detachment to invade the kingdom of Naples. With difficulty Pescara persuaded his colleagues to neglect this remoter danger and to concentrate on the immediate purpose of defeating the main enemy[3]. On the arrival of reinforcements from Germany the imperial commander took the field, broke into the French camp at Pavia, and destroyed an army which a few months before had been in a position to overwhelm him.

The victory of Pavia marked the arrival of a

[1] This campaign, like that of the Garigliano, renders comprehensible Machiavelli's well-known remark that the French were most formidable at the first impetus—if withstood or avoided they became demoralized by hardships and as weak as women (*Ritratti delle cose della Francia, Opere*, vol. vi, p. 297).

[2] Du Bellay, *Mémoires*, bk. ii, notes this as the fatal blunder.

[3] Nardi, *Istorie della città di Firenze* (ed. Gelli), bk. vii, § 19; Du Bellay, *loc. cit.*

strategic method which became traditional in the imperial service. We can see the tradition being formed in the campaigns which crushed the final effort of the French monarchy to make good its Italian claims. Here again a clear-sighted pursuit of a single strategic objective triumphs over the disconnected manoeuvring and the ill-calculated attacks of a past generation. In the Neapolitan campaign of 1527–8 the imperial army, unprepared for a decision in the field, withdrew into the capital before the advance of Lautrec. During the subsequent siege the sea communications of the garrison were severely restricted by the Venetian and the Genoese allies of France. Time, however, worked against the French. Sickness decimated their army, and the slow workings of diplomacy mitigated the rigour of the sea-blockade. The merit of the imperial command consists in the advantage it took of this change of conditions. The necessity for the "final blow" was never lost sight of. Whereas a leader of the school of Prospero Colonna would have been content to trust to diplomacy and climate to complete the discomfiture of the enemy, the prince of Orange made continual sorties against the French, cut their communications with the Venetian fleet[1], and finally, when they were in the act of abandoning the siege, delivered an assault which turned their retreat into a rout[2]. In the same way Antonio de Leyva, who

[1] Guicciardini, *Istoria d' Italia*, bk. XIX.
[2] This attack was not a mere sortie producing a rearguard action, but a bid for a decision which succeeded. The French rearguard, consisting of picked troops—the celebrated Tuscan

withstood St Pol in Lombardy, sheltered himself in fortresses until he was reinforced and until lack of money and the diversion of troops against Genoa had diminished the numbers of the French. He then issued from his defences, made a surprise attack on St Pol at Landriano, broke his army and took him prisoner. In both these campaigns the imperial commanders follow very closely the strategical principles of the marquis of Pescara and of Gonsalvo de Cordova. When we remember that at this time the soldiers of the emperor were trailing their pikes over the length and breadth of Europe, and that the methods of the imperial captains were becoming a pattern to the world, only then can we begin to gauge the debt which modern strategy owes to the two great leaders who were the architects of the Hapsburg power in Italy.

Black Band—was first attacked and routed. Then the French main body was assailed and put to flight, and Pedro Navarro, the ablest surviving French commander, brought back a prisoner to Naples (see Segni, *Storie Fiorentine*, bk. II).

CHAPTER III

INFANTRY

N ICCOLÒ Machiavelli, writing in the second decade of the sixteenth century, describes the
infantry as "the substance and sinew of an army,
and that part of it which ought constantly to be
most considered[1]." These words sum up the rise in
the status of the footsoldier which began with the
victories of the English and the Swiss, and which
culminated in the Italian wars. The change was a
double one. In the first place it was the evolution of
a dominant type of infantry for the whole of Europe.
National infantries, as we have seen, arose in the
fifteenth century, but these differed very considerably in equipment, in organization, and in tactics.
During the Italian wars, however, when composite
armies were the rule, when it was possible, for instance, for Cesare Borgia to incorporate into a single
unit Swiss, Germans, Gascons, and Italians[2], and when
the enemies of one campaign might be allies in the
next, it was inevitable that competition between
divergent methods and exchange of ideas between
varying nationalities should tend to standardize the

[1] Machiavelli, *Discorsi*, bk. II, ch. XVIII (trans. N. H. Thomson).
[2] Machiavelli, *Legazione XI*, doc. 81.

profession of arms[1]. In this way arose for the first time a European infantry[2], and as infantry became less a local and more a European thing, so the mediaeval contempt for unmounted troops began to disappear. To some extent indeed the footsoldier succeeded to the international position which had formerly been held by the mailed knight. The other aspect of this same development was an extension of the activities of the footsoldier owing to the improvement and the rapid multiplication of portable firearms. Not only did the infantryman at last attain a uniformly honourable standing in all European armies, but his sphere of usefulness was at the same time permanently widened. He became the most important factor in every battle. To recur to the words of Machiavelli, he became not merely that part of an army which should be "most considered," but its very "substance and sinew."

The increased reputation which infantry acquired was due mainly to the Swiss: its increased versatility was due mainly to the Spaniards. The reputation of the Swiss was established before the opening of the Italian wars; on the other hand the contribution of the Spaniards to the development of the infantry arm

[1] The battle of Ravenna affords perhaps the most striking example of the cosmopolitan character of the armies which fought in the Italian wars. On the French side there were French, Germans, Swiss, Navarrese, Italians, and Greeks: on the Spanish side there were Spaniards, Italians, Sicilians, Greeks from Naples and from across the Adriatic, Tyrrhene islanders, and Africans (see Porto, *Lettere Storiche*, no. 66, and Champier, *Les Gestes de Bayard*, bk. II, ch. IX).

[2] Rüstow, *Geschichte der Infanterie*, vol. I, bk. III, pp. 197–201.

was made gradually during the course of those wars and its full effect was not seen till their closing years. Thus, in point of time, the Spaniards may be regarded as in some measure adapting and carrying on the work of the Swiss. It is well, however, to insist on the originality and the permanence of the Swiss contribution. One feature they introduced into European warfare—to wit, the manoeuvring of pikemen in close formation—which remained unaltered for two centuries. The extension of the use of small arms by the Spaniards was of even more enduring importance, but it was quite strictly an addition to, rather than a supersession of, the teaching of the Swiss. In the present chapter we shall consider first the influence of Swiss tactics as practised in Italy; next will follow an examination of the progressive employment of firearms by the Spaniards; we shall then be in a position to note the evolution of that combination of pike and musket which subsequently became normal to the infantry of all countries.

The pike, a long wooden shaft with a sharp iron head, appears to have originated in the Netherlands before the twelfth century[1]. It was valuable chiefly as a defensive weapon against hostile cavalry, and its general restriction to a defensive rôle prevented it from becoming in the Middle Ages as popular an infantry weapon as the crossbow of the Italians or the longbow of the English. These two latter weapons, however, had only a very limited power of offence. Archers were incapable of shock tactics. Their worth,

[1] Oman, *Art of War in the Middle Ages*, p. 374.

and indeed their survival, depended on their ability to injure the heavy cavalry of the enemy while keeping beyond its reach. It was by these methods that the English won their victories in the Hundred Years' War[1]. In the fifteenth century the Swiss introduced a revolutionary change into the art of war by evolving a shock tactic for unmounted troops. They armed themselves at first chiefly with the halberd[2] (a shaft eight feet long carrying a hatchet blade as well as a spike at one end), and formed themselves into compact squares which were trained to move swiftly without breaking their formation[3]. These battalions were thus capable not only of presenting a formidable obstacle to a charge of cavalry, but also of advancing upon and breaking up any less compact body of men. As the Swiss gained experience they adopted the pike as their principal weapon. Although the pike was a simple thrusting weapon, whereas the halberd served both for thrusting and striking, it nevertheless proved itself a better defence against cavalry. This was due to its greater length[4] and to its very simplicity of design, which enabled the outer ranks of pikemen to cross the projecting heads of their weapons and thus to present to the enemy an impenetrable barrier of steel points. This custom of

[1] Oman, *Art of War in the Middle Ages*, pp. 612–13, 629; Duparcq, *L'art de la guerre*, vol. II, ch. I, § 3.

[2] Rüstow, *Geschichte der Infanterie*, vol. I, bk. II, p. 163.

[3] Oman, *Art of War in the Middle Ages* (Lothian Essay), p. 66.

[4] About 10 feet in 1494 according to Rüstow, vol. I, pp. 216–17.

crossing pikes grew to be normal in both attack[1] and defence[2]. Most of the Swiss dispensed with body-armour and shields for the sake of increased mobility, but continued to carry swords[3] and daggers[4]. There was always a proportion of missile weapons. By the last decade of the fifteenth century these seem to have consisted almost entirely of firearms. The men who carried them formed about one-tenth of the total numbers[5] and were employed as skirmishers to open the fight[6]. They were a subsidiary arm unable of themselves to exert a decisive influence on the fortunes of the day.

Such was the organization of the Swiss infantry at the time of Charles VIII's expedition. Their prestige at that time may be estimated from the fact that the infantry of all the other nations with which they came in contact in Italy, except that of the Italians themselves, had in a greater or less degree already adopted the same organization. The German landsknechts differed from the Swiss in no important particular[7]. They had a smaller proportion of firearms and were even less disposed to carry armour and shields, but otherwise their resemblance to the Swiss was so marked that contemporary Italian writers often fail

[1] *E.g.* the Swiss at Marignano (Barrillon, *Journal*, ch. I).
[2] *E.g.* the Spanish at Ravenna (Loyal Serviteur, *Histoire de Bayart*, ch. LIV).
[3] Rüstow, *Geschichte der Infanterie*, vol. I, bk. III, p. 215).
[4] Jähns, *Handbuch*, p. 1056.
[5] Giovio, *Istorie*, bk. II.
[6] *Relazioni of the Venetian Ambassadors*, Series I, vol. VI, pp. 16 *seq.*
[7] *Ibid.*

to distinguish between them. The French and Gascon infantry were modelled on the Swiss in their formation but were neither so well drilled nor so effective in battle[1]. Since indeed the Gascons consisted chiefly of crossbowmen they could not be expected to fit well into a formation designed primarily for shock tactics, and their being so organized is more important as an indication of Swiss influence than as an actual military development. Gonsalvo de Cordova had borrowed largely from the Swiss in his reform of the Spanish army[2]. He armed half his infantry with light pikes, one-sixth with firearms, and the remainder with sword and dagger only. Little or no armour was worn, but a round shield protected those who carried neither pikes nor firearms. The Spanish infantrymen, like the Swiss and the Germans, were designed for offensive action. The battle was opened in the same way by small parties of skirmishers; then pikemen and swordsmen advanced in mass formation, the pikemen broke the enemy's front, and the swordsmen pushed their way into the gaps and completed his disorganization. In contrast to France and Spain, the Italian states were singularly uninfluenced by the military opinion which emanated from Switzerland[3]. For fighting in the field the footsoldier was still despised[4]. He skirmished in open order with his crossbow and left hand-to-hand combat to the

[1] Guicciardini, *Istoria d' Italia*, bk. I, p. 121; Giovio, *Istorie*, bk. xv.

[2] Jähns, *Handbuch*, p. 1044.

[3] Giovio, *Istorie*, bk. II, p. 32.

[4] *Ibid.*

cavalry. He was unacquainted with the halberd[1].
Firearms were regarded as a novelty of very doubtful
value[2]. Many rulers still encouraged the practice of
archery on appointed days[3].

The general result of the mingling of these various
infantries on the battlefields of Italy was a still closer
all-round approximation to the Swiss type. The
crossbow gradually became extinct. It became associated with the less disciplined class of infantry, and
was employed chiefly in the defence of obstacles, as,
for instance, at the siege of Padua in 1509, where it
is said to have inflicted severe punishment on the
unprotected Germans[4]. Crossbowmen played an
effective part at Marignano in 1515[5], but there again
they were stationed behind ramparts, and in spite of
their success they were not used for important work
in any subsequent battle.

The uninterrupted success of Charles VIII's invasion of Naples and his easy repulse of superior
forces at Fornovo impressed the Italians with a sense
of their own military deficiencies. To the condottiere
Vitellozzo Vitelli belongs the honour of being the
first to organize Italian infantry on the Swiss plan[6].
Cesare Borgia conscripted and drilled native troops

[1] The halberds of Charles VIII's army were a novelty to
the Italians: see Passero, *Giornali*, p. 71; Giovio, *Istorie*,
bk. II, p. 28.
[2] Cf. Machiavelli, *Arte della guerra*, bk. II.
[3] Cf. Diario Ferrarese, 24 May 1496.
[4] Porto, *Lettere Storiche*, no. 31.
[5] Giovio, *Istorie*, bk. XV; Vegius, *Historia*, anno 1515,
p. 16.
[6] Giovio, *Elogi*, bk. IV.

in the same way for his wars in Romagna[1]. But the
most elaborate attempt to form an efficient Italian
infantry was made by Florence. This attempt grew
out of the war with Pisa which lasted from 1495 to
1509. Having tried in vain to conquer Pisa first with
mercenary and afterwards with allied help, the Florentine government decided that a permanent standing army would alone be equal to the task. The
enrolment and organization of this force were due
chiefly to the faith and enthusiasm of Machiavelli;
by 1506 it numbered 10,000 men and the expense
and effort were justified by the eventual submission
of the revolted city. The feature of greatest interest
in the Florentine militia is the subordination of
cavalry to infantry. For the Pisan war Florence did
not raise any native cavalry at all. The army of
10,000 men which won the war was an army of infantry with a few hired horsemen added as an
auxiliary arm. Next it should be noted that the
formation adopted was the massed battalion, that
these battalions were exercised regularly in a system
of drill copied from the Swiss, and that they were
officered by professional soldiers acquainted with
Swiss or German methods of warfare[2]. A further
significant point is the distribution of weapons.
Seventy men in every hundred were pikemen; the
remainder carried swords, daggers, crossbows, or firearms[3]. There is no better evidence of the military
efficiency of the Swiss than this conscious imitation

---

[1] Canestrini, *Scritti inediti di Machiavelli*, p. xxxvi.
[2] *Ibid.* p. xlvi.   [3] *Ibid.* p. 342.

of them by a state which contained the acutest minds of the age.

From the Swiss who fought for France in Naples several useful lessons were learnt by the soldiers of the Great Captain. Finding their own light pike inferior in battle to that of the Swiss they promptly adopted a heavier weapon[1]. This process of substitution had not been completed at the time of Gonsalvo's retirement to Barletta, and it was partly for this reason that he refused to take the field until the arrival of the more suitably armed landsknechts[2]. The halberd was not adopted by the Spaniards. They judged their own sword and buckler more effective for hand-to-hand fighting, and their decision was justified by later events. At Ravenna in 1512, when for the first time Spaniard and German met in pitched battle, the agility of the Spanish swordsmen and the protection of their shields enabled them to penetrate beneath the opposing pikes, and to cut a way deep into the battalions of the enemy[3]. On this occasion fortune robbed the Spaniards of the victory which was their due, but by the time they marched unbroken from the field they had done enough to sap the faith of the world in the invincibility of the Swiss formation.

Even before Ravenna the more discerning must have recognized that there were limits to the capabilities of the Germans and Swiss. Their tactics

[1] Giovio, *Istorie*, bk. III, p. 58.
[2] Giovio, *Vita Consalvi Cordubae*, bk. II.
[3] Guicciardini, *Istoria d' Italia*, bk. x; Machiavelli, *Prince*, ch. XXVI.

required open country. Their huge squares, which
often contained 10,000 men[1], could not be formed
up on narrow or broken ground, and the fact that
they were equally defensible on every side tended to
make their commanders impatient of natural or artificial protection. But occasions arose, especially in
assaulting or defending towns, when they could not
employ their peculiar formation. On these occasions
they proved unable to adapt themselves to the new
conditions, and, rather than try to think out methods
of meeting an unaccustomed situation, they sometimes refused to take part in siege warfare[2]. In consequence the opinion gained ground that the Swiss,
though unconquerable in the field, were not fitted
for the defence or storming of obstacles[3], and thus
their own conservatism—an unpardonable crime in
exponents of the art of war—began to undermine the
prestige of the most famous infantrymen in Europe.
The Swiss themselves introduced only one small
change during the Italian wars, namely, the length-
ening of the pike from ten feet in 1494 to eighteen
feet in 1520[4]. Even this change was open to ob-

[1] As at Marignano (see Francis I's Letter to the duchesse
d'Angoulesme); and cf. the Venetian ambassador's description
of the German infantry in 1507 (*Relazioni*, Series I, vol. VI,
pp. 16 *seq.*).
[2] *E.g.* at Novara in 1522 (Du Bellay, *Mémoires*, bk. II, p.
219).
[3] Cf. Barrillon, *Journal*, ch. I, p. 132; Prato, *De rebus
mediolanensibus*, p. 345; Specianus, *De bello gallico*, bk. II,
p. 138; Machiavelli, *Ritratti delle cose della Francia* (*Opere,*
vol. VI, p. 297).
[4] A step in this process is seen in Vitellozzo Vitelli's victory
at Soriano in 1497 (see Guicciardini, *Istoria d' Italia*, bk. III).

jection. The advantage of greater reach was counter-balanced by increased unwieldiness, and, though most infantry commanders adopted it as an improve-ment, the Spaniards refused to make an alteration which threatened their mobility.

In truth mobility, with its corollary, adaptability, was the special virtue of the Spaniard. He cultivated speed not only in his practice of the art of war but also in his treatment of its problems. While the Swiss and the Germans were married to their rigid system of tactics and shut their eyes to its proved inadequacies, the Spaniard remained an adventurer in military matters. He knew that in war no system is infallible and no difficulty insoluble, and he seized every opportunity which the Italian wars offered him to experiment, to improve, and, in a word, to win. The most important result of this mental and physical resiliency was the development of the use of firearms by the footsoldier.

At the end of the fifteenth century the distinction between small arms and artillery had not yet been made. There existed a small, very portable type of firearm which was unmistakably an infantry arm, but there also existed a heavier variety of the same weapon which was carried on the march by beasts of burden[1] and sometimes mounted for action[2]. The lighter weapon was seldom more than four feet long, and sometimes as short as three feet; the heavier

[1] *E.g.* in the Swiss army which invaded Milan in 1511 (see Guicciardini, *Istoria d' Italia*, bk. x).

[2] *E.g.* by Pedro Navarro at Ravenna in 1512 (see Coccinius, *De bellis italicis*, p. 226).

weapon frequently reached the length of five feet. This heavier weapon was usually fitted with a hook by the use of which the footsoldier was the better able to support its weight and the shock of its discharge. With the exception of this device there was no important difference in design between the larger and the smaller of the portable firearms. Each consisted of an iron barrel and a sunken wooden butt. Each fired leaden balls which were discharged by the introduction of a slow-match into a powder-hole at the side[1]. In each case the sighting was very rough, but in the case of the larger weapon it was accurate enough for a careful shot from the walls of a beleaguered town to bring down a hostile commander engaged in reconnaissance well beyond the outer ditch[2]. The Italians usually distinguished the smaller and the larger weapon by the respective names "schioppetto" and "archibugio" (or "archibuso"). Other nations drew no such clear distinction. The terms "arquebuse" and "hakbut" (Hakenbüchse), which correspond to the Italian "archibugio," were applied to hand firearms of all sizes; French writers, however, frequently indicate the larger type by the words "arquebuse à croc" (or "arquebuse à crochet"). This confusion prevents the inquirer from reaching any definite conclusions as to the distribution of the two classes of firearms within the infantry forma-

[1] In these details I follow Rüstow, *Geschichte der Infanterie*, vol. I, bk. III, pp. 220, 225, and Jähns, *Handbuch*, pp. 780 *seq.*

[2] *E.g.* Pitigliano at Novara, 1495 (Benedetti, *Il fatto d' arme del Tarro*, bk. II) and Lorenzo de' Medici at Mondolfo, 1517 (Guicciardini, *Istoria d' Italia*, bk. XIII).

tions. In the pages which follow the word "arquebus" will be used to describe indiscriminately infantry firearms of all sizes, and the same general
character will attach to the meaning of the word
"arquebusier."

We have seen that the Swiss regarded firearms as
an auxiliary to the pike. Only one-tenth of those who
served under Charles VIII were arquebusiers[1]. This
same proportion was maintained in theory by Florence when the new militia was organized in 1506,
though it is probable that in practice the ratio was
even less[2]. According to the Venetian ambassador
writing from Germany in 1507 firearms were still
more neglected by the landsknechts, since in a company of 400 men there were as a rule only 25 arquebusiers[3]. The proportion of one in ten seems to have
been customary among the Italian infantry serving
in the Venetian army in the year 1510[4]. Nevertheless there are indications that the number of arquebuses was increasing slowly but steadily throughout
the first two decades of the Italian wars. Particularly
striking is the ratio of firearms to pikes in the Swiss
army which invaded Milan in 1511[5]. One man in
every four carried an arquebus, and the arquebusiers
were more than usually active in the skirmishes which
took place during the abortive march of the invaders.

[1] Giovio, *Istorie*, bk. II.
[2] Canestrini, *Scritti inediti di Machiavelli*, pp. 325, xxxix.
[3] *Relazioni of Venetian Ambassadors*, Series I, vol. VI, pp.
16 *seq.*
[4] Porto, *Lettere Storiche*, no. 52.
[5] Guicciardini, *Istoria d' Italia*, bk. IX.

In view of this unusual activity and of the fact that
the proportion of firearms was subsequently reduced,
it is not perhaps fanciful to conjecture that the composition of the army was in the nature of an experiment. If this was the case we may conclude that
diffidence was one of the motives which prevented
the Swiss from challenging a decision. The spread of
the use of firearms to the civilian population about
this time also provides evidence that their number
was increasing. A letter from Friuli, written in 1510,
describes the people of that country as experts in the
use of the arquebus[1], while the innumerable peasants
who fought for Venice at the battle of Vicenza in
1514 are reported to have been well supplied with the
same weapon[2]. The fact that the emperor's German
arquebusiers were criticized in the year 1510 for their
inexperience in the use of their weapons seems likewise to point to the extension of small arms among
new classes of troops[3].

Already before 1494 the Spanish army had shown
an exceptional appreciation of the importance of

[1] Porto, *Lettere Storiche*, no. 44. The word used is "schioppio."

[2] Guicciardini, *Istoria d' Italia*, bk. xi. The Venetian
peasantry seems to have been well supplied with small firearms as early as 1495. Cf. Sanuto, *La spedizione di Carlo VIII*,
bk. ii, p. 378: "fatto le mostre di schiopetieri erano nel paese
nostro, zoè villani;...et quelli volesse esser a tal exercitio
fusseno exempti de ogni angaria personal; tamen al tempo di
guerra fusseno ubligati di andar in campo; et questo è di
numero 8000." Nevertheless these "schiopetieri" were not
held in very high repute: cf. the letter of a Governador of the
Venetian camp, cited by Sanuto (*loc. cit.* p. 404), in which
occurs the significant phrase: "cavalli 5500 et zerca pedoni
6000, il resto cernide et guastadori, schiopetieri etc."

[3] Porto, *Lettere Storiche*, no. 54.

small arms. Gonsalvo de Cordova armed one-sixth of
his infantry with arquebuses[1], and this high proportion was justified by the superiority which it gave
his troops in the early campaigns in Naples. This
superiority was manifested not so much in the open
field, where the reputation of the Swiss was fully
maintained, but rather in ambushes and the defence
of obstacles—operations to which the Swiss and the
Germans refused to adapt themselves. The inelas-
ticity of the Swiss military method was thus the
Spaniards' opportunity, and it is from this point of
view that we must consider the rise of firearms if we
wish to seize its full significance. Two events which
occurred during the campaign of 1502–3 foreshadow
the coming importance of the arquebusier. The first
is the successful defence of Canosa by Pedro Navarro
against the French under Nemours. With a garrison
of about 700 men, of whom 200 were arquebusiers,
he sustained a three-days bombardment, which practically destroyed the walls of the town, and repulsed
a series of almost hourly assaults made by greatly
superior numbers of the enemy. So determined was
the defence that when at last the position of the
garrison became no longer tenable the French commander allowed them to march out with the honours
of war and marvelled as he watched them depart
that so few should have been able to withstand so
many[2]. The other instance of the value of the Spanish

---

[1] Jähns, *Handbuch*, p. 1044.

[2] Giovio, *Vita Consalvi Cordubae*, bk. II. D'Auton, *Chroniques
de Louis XII*, 1502, ch. XI, also describes this defence: though
a French writer he presents the feat of the Spanish garrison

arquebusier is a sortie made by the garrison of Barletta against the rear of Nemours' army as it was marching to Canosa. A small force of arquebusiers with cavalry to support them overtook the enemy, extended on his flanks, and kept up a heavy fire which caused considerable loss[1]. These two examples are cited not because the obstinate defence of towns or successful skirmishes were new things, but because such operations had usually been left by the Swiss and the Germans to the despised Italian or Gascon crossbowmen, who alone possessed in sufficient quantity the necessary missile weapons. Now, however, an army is coming to the front which not only rivals the Swiss in their own tactics, but is also developing a light infantry which will be able ultimately to turn the scales of battle.

During the Neapolitan campaigns of the Great Captain and the twelve following years—years in which, as we have seen, the proportion of arquebusiers among the Swiss, the Germans, and the Italians was steadily, if slowly, increasing—the rôle of the hand firearm seems to have been confined almost entirely to the defence of obstacles. The battle of Cerignola in 1503 is the successful defence of an entrenched camp against massed pikemen. It is noteworthy because the defence was largely the work of Spanish arquebusiers, and because the unsuccessful assault was in every way a normal Swiss

in an even more brilliant light by making the bombardment last five days and a half. He gives the numbers of the garrison as 1200 at the opening of the siege and 900 at its close.

[1] Giovio, *loc. cit.*

attack—two facts which deserve particular emphasis[1].
The prolonged resistance in the same year of the town
of Ceri to the army of Cesare Borgia was due in great
part to the skilful use of arquebuses[2], and an eyewitness testifies to their employment in large numbers
at the successful defence of Padua against Maximilian in 1509[3]. The Venetian garrison of Brescia
contained 1500 arquebusiers in the year 1512[4].
Three years later the same city was gallantly defended throughout three sieges by Spanish and German troops who were well supplied with firearms[5].
The arquebusier played an important part in the repulse of Alviano from the walls of Verona in 1513[6].
The three important battles of these same years—
Ravenna, Novara, and Marignano—all took the form
of an assault on an entrenched camp and show a
growing tendency on the part of the defenders to
rely on small arms. At Ravenna the Spaniards protected themselves with arquebuses mounted on
wagons, but failed by this means to prevent the
Germans from forcing a way into their position[7]. At
Novara the Swiss sustained heavy losses from the

[1] Giovio, *loc. cit.* It is also noteworthy that the death of
Nemours, the French commander, was due to arquebus fire.
D'Auton says he was pierced by three arquebus shots (*Chroni-
ques de Louis XII*, 1503, ch. 11).

[2] Giustinian, *Dispaccio* no. 313.

[3] "y pleuvoient les coups de hacquebute" (Loyal Serviteur,
Histoire de Bayart, ch. XXXIII); cf. also Mocenico, *La guerra
di Cambrai*, bk. II.

[4] Floranges, *Mémoires*, vol. I, p. 81 (in the edition published
by the Société de l'histoire de France).

[5] Giovio, *Istorie*, bk. XVI.   [6] *Ibid.* bk. XI.

[7] Coccinius, *De bellis italicis.*

German arquebuses and were unable to achieve victory until they had put them out of action[1]. At Marignano the French arquebusiers and crossbowmen developed a continuous and formidable volume of fire by discharging their weapons in rotation[2] and inflicting such heavy casualties on the Swiss that the arquebus may be said on that day to have first challenged the supremacy of the pike.

The peace of Noyon, signed in 1516, marks the end of the first stage in the arrival of the portable firearm. The example of the Spaniards had led to its adoption in an increased degree by the armies of other nations, but its diffusion was slow and its function mainly defensive. The reopening of the war in 1521 marks the beginning of a further and more rapid development. Once more the original influence comes from Spain. This time it takes the form of a new invention. In the first campaign the Spaniards brought into the field a larger and improved firearm which came to be called the musket[3]. It was six feet long and fired balls weighing two ounces[4]. Its weight necessitated the use of a fork-shaped rest[5], but its

---

[1] Floranges, *Mémoires*, vol. I, p. 126. The German arquebusiers were 800 strong.

[2] Giovio, *Istorie*, bk. xv.

[3] First used at the siege of Parma 1521 (Du Bellay, *Mémoires*, bk. II, p. 189).

[4] Rüstow, *Geschichte der Infanterie*, vol. I, bk. III, pp. 221–5.

[5] The forked rest was not unknown before the invention of the musket. *E.g.* the fifty picked infantrymen who accompanied Pedro Navarro at the battle of Ravenna (1512) carried "archibusi grossi, ma facilmente portabili coll' aiuto d' alcuni sostegni a guisa di gruccie o forche di ferro fitti in terra" (Nardi, *Istorie della città di Firenze*, bk. v, § 35). On the other

unwieldiness was compensated for by its great killing-power—its ability to bring down two armoured cavalrymen with one shot. For a long time this new weapon was classed as an arquebus, and it is therefore difficult to trace its rate of increase[1]. Occasionally it is referred to as a part of the artillery owing to its being transported by horses on the march[2]. Nevertheless, in spite of this confusion, three facts are quite plain. The musket was multiplied continuously, though in some places slowly (for instance, Florence possessed only sixty in 1527)[3]; its effectiveness, particularly in the hands of the Spaniards, impressed the military opinion of Europe; and, as a consequence, the manufacture of small arms, both arquebuses and muskets, received a new impetus.

In these later years really large bodies of infantry with firearms begin to appear in the armies of the different belligerents. For example, in 1521 Prospero Colonna's garrison at Milan was estimated at 40,000: of these 9000 were Spanish arquebusiers[4]. Again, in 1527 the duke of Urbino's army was estimated at 29,000: of these 10,000 were Italian arquebusiers[5].

hand this passage may refer to the use of the musket at a period earlier than it is commonly supposed to have existed. It is noteworthy that the special weapon referred to was placed in the hands of a few selected men.

[1] Cf. Jähns, *Handbuch*, pp. 1055–6.

[2] Cf. *Relazioni of the Venetian Ambassadors*, Series II, vol. I, pp. 9 *seq.* [3] *Ibid.*

[4] Joseph ben Joshua ben Meir, *Chronicles* (trans. C. H. F. Bialloblotzky), para. 615. The figures are probably exaggerated —at any rate they include armed citizens—but the ratio is significant.

[5] Guicciardini, *Istoria d' Italia*, bk. XVIII.

In this same year we find the prince of Orange commanding two companies which consist entirely of arquebusiers[1]—a type of force hitherto formed for special purposes only[2]. Among the Swiss and the Germans the proportion of firearms did not rise so rapidly as among the Spanish and the Italians. That there was nevertheless a very marked increase is proved by the fact that one-eighth of the Germans who sacked Rome in 1527 were arquebusiers[3]: in 1510, as we have already noted, the usual German proportion had been one-sixteenth[4]. Furthermore, the presence in 1528 of 400 musketeers among Brunswick's 10,000 foot[5] indicates that the northern peoples were paying due attention to the most modern of the many types of firearm. Even Machiavelli, who had little faith in the military value of gunpowder, was compelled by the facts which he saw around him to recommend in 1521 that one-sixth of every infantry formation should be armed with the arquebus[6].

As we should expect from this rapid diffusion of the infantry firearm, its ability to defend obstacles was tested more and more in the later years of the Italian wars. At the siege of Parma in 1521—the first important siege of the new war which began in

[1] Guicciardini, *Istoria d' Italia*, bk. XVII.

[2] Canestrini, *Scritti inediti di Machiavelli*, p. xli.

[3] 1500 Handschützen among 12,000 Landsknechte (Reisner, *Historia und Beschreibung Herrn Georgen von Frundsberg*, pp. 86, 88).

[4] See p. 41 above.

[5] Guicciardini, *Istoria d' Italia*, bk. XIX.

[6] *Arte della guerra*, bk. II.

that year—the arquebusiers of the French army successfully defended a city-wall which was unprotected
by a ditch[1]. At Novara in 1522 the imperial garrison
developed formidable arquebus-fire from trenches
dug on the flanks of the breach[2]. At Cremona in 1523
the arquebusiers of the defence loopholed the walls
of houses commanding the scene of the assault[3]. At
Marseilles in 1524 the besiegers were unable to assault
the breach they had made owing to the veritable
deluge of bullets which received them when they attempted to approach[4]. At Pavia in 1524 it was
largely due to the efficiency of the imperial arquebusiers that Francis I was compelled to adopt the
slow, and in this case fatal, expedient of beleaguering
the city[5]. In 1527–8 Neapolitan towns, such as Melfi[6]
and Forcha di Penne[7], which a generation before had
surrendered to Charles VIII without a blow, received
the French invader with a murderous hail of lead and
were reduced only at the cost of very severe casualties.

It was, however, not in siege warfare but in open
fighting that there occurred the final and most important development in the use of small arms. In
the closing phase of the Italian wars the arquebusier

[1] Du Bellay, *Mémoires*, bk. II, p. 189.
[2] *Ibid.* p. 219.
[3] Specianus, *De bello gallico*, bk. II (in Ceruti's *Biblioth.
Hist. It.*).
[4] Giovio, *Vita Marchionis Piscariae*, bk. IV.
[5] Du Bellay, *Mémoires*, bk. II, p. 325.
[6] Guicciardini, *Istoria d' Italia*, bk. XVIII; Du Bellay,
Mémoires, bk. III, p. 70.
[7] Monluc, *Mémoires*, bk. I. This place is in the Abruzzi.

emerges from behind his rampart and takes the field
with his weapon as his only protection. He is utilized
by a skilful leader in almost every kind of operation,
and the result is the evolution of a light infantry
worthy to rank in military value with the battalions
of serried pikes. This momentous advance in the art
of war was due chiefly to the genius of the marquis
of Pescara. The mind which directed the strategy of
the campaign of Pavia was engaged during the preceding years in perfecting the instrument with which
that campaign was won.

An instance of an orderly and disciplined offensive
by arquebusiers—an offensive distinct, that is to say,
from mere skirmishing—had occurred as early as 1512
at the storming of Brescia by Gaston de Foix. On
that occasion the storming party consisted of 500
dismounted men-at-arms followed closely by a large
body of arquebusiers. At a word of command given
from time to time the men-at-arms crouched and the
arquebusiers fired over their heads[1]. This provision
of a human rampart for men who had been accustomed to shelter themselves behind obstacles shows
the tentative nature of an experiment which by its
success invited repetition. The very effective alterna-
tion of fire from the French arquebuses at Marignano
(1515)[2] is another early example of the training of
arquebusiers in definite battle tactics. During the
interval of comparative peace which lasted from 1516

[1] Porto, *Lettere Storiche*, no. 65; Anselmi, *Descrittione del sacco di Brescia.*
[2] Giovio, *Istorie*, bk. xv.

to 1521 the Spanish army added to the military value
of the infantry firearm not only by adopting the new
invention of the musket, but also by studying carefully the question of its tactical employment. When
the war began again the ascendancy of the Spanish
arquebusiers and musketeers over those of other
nations soon became very marked, and their bold
handling by the marquis of Pescara foreshadowed
almost from the first the ultimate victory of the imperial arms.

It was the imperial arquebusiers who, during Prospero Colonna's retirement from Rebecco in 1521,
repulsed with heavy loss an attack on the rearguard
by the pursuing French[1]. Later in the same year at
the famous crossing of the Adda at Vauri these same
arquebusiers saved a situation which threatened at
one time to end in disaster. When a strong counterattack menaced with annihilation the first small
crossing party, a picked detachment of Pescara's men
was hurried over to stiffen the resistance. French
men-at-arms were unseated and Gascon crossbowmen
outranged by the vigorous arquebus-fire to which
they were now subjected, and, under cover of this
temporary check to the enemy, the area of the landing
was widened and a bridgehead secured[2]. At the battle
of Bicocca in the following year the value of infantry
firearms was first demonstrated on a large scale. The
front of the imperial army, which was protected by
a sunken road, consisted of four ranks of arquebusiers, mainly Spanish, with German pikemen massed

[1] Giovio, *Vita Marchionis Piscariae*, bk. II.   [2] *Ibid.*

immediately behind them. The arquebusiers were in-
structed by Pescara to hold their fire until the advancing Swiss were at close range; then, when he
gave the signal, each rank was to shoot in turn and
to reload in a kneeling posture in order to leave a
clear field of fire for the ranks behind[1]. Arquebuses
were also posted among the ripe crops flanking the
road[2] and in a position commanding a bridge which
gave entrance to the rear of the encampment[3]. These
arrangements were entirely successful. Both the
Swiss, who attacked the imperialists frontally, and
the French cavalry, who tried to rush the bridge,
were mown down in great numbers and forced to
retire. From this day forth the arquebus and the
musket rank equally in warfare with the lance and
the pike, and the army which neglected firearms gave
odds to the enemy.

Having demonstrated to the world the excellence
of the new infantry tactic, the imperial service did
not imitate the Swiss in like circumstances by proceeding at once to standardize its discovery. The
marquis of Pescara and his captains looked less to
the achievement of the past than to the promise of
the future. Without delay they sought to develop
and to exploit what they had discovered. They were
animated by the same eager spirit which was at this
time carrying the Latin civilization over the con-
tinent of America. On the very field of Bicocca a new
use for the hand firearm suggested itself to the fierce

[1] Giovio, *Vita Marchionis Piscariae*, bk. II.
[2] Guicciardini, *Istoria d' Italia*, bk. XIV.
[3] Giovio, *Vita Marchionis Piscariae*, bk. II.

young Italian condottiere who covered the French retreat. Giovanni de' Medici, who undertook this task with a mixed force of cavalry and arquebusiers, found his movements hampered by the slowness of his unmounted troops. Hitherto such a difficulty had been overcome on special occasions by mounting infantry on the crupper behind light cavalry[1]. Taught by his experience at Bicocca, Giovanni now began to mount a proportion of arquebusiers on horses of little value and to mix them with his cavalry; when they came into action they dismounted and fought as foot-soldiers[2]. He thus evolved a genuine mounted infantry—a force combining the equipment and tactical value of light infantry with the mobility of light cavalry. This force he incorporated into his "Black Band" of choice Tuscan youth, and to it we may perhaps partly attribute that readiness of his famous command for "anything hot and unwholesome" which has been characteristic of the mounted infantries of more recent times.

Two years later an opportunity occurred for thoroughly testing the powers of the new light troops. The battle of the Sesia[3] was a blow struck at a

[1] This practice was resorted to by the raiders who tried to capture Pitigliano at the opening of the Cambrai War in 1509 (Bembo, *Istoria Viniziana da lui volgarizzata*, bk. VII), by the Venetians in their abortive attempt on Brescia in 1512 (*ibid.* bk. XII), and by the Spanish and German troops who defended Brescia in 1516 (Giovio, *Istorie*, bk. XVI).

[2] Rossi, *Vita di Giovanni de' Medici*, p. 211.

[3] Best described by Giovio, *Vita Marchionis Piscariae*, bk. III. Champier, *Gestes de Bayard*, bk. III, ch. VII, emphasizes the deadly effect of the imperial arquebuses.

retreating and distressed enemy by a force of cavalry
and mobile infantry. Arquebusiers were rushed forward by Pescara and Giovanni de' Medici on the
cruppers of the cavalry, on their own horses, and on
foot. A devastating fire from flank and rear was
poured into the French army. The French men-at-
arms charged the elusive foe in vain. Neither in
accuracy nor in rapidity of fire were the Swiss arquebusiers a match for the imperialists. A large body of
Swiss pikemen which attempted to beat off the
pursuit was surrounded and annihilated. When at
last the remnant of the beaten army escaped, it was
with the loss of much of its artillery. Arquebus shots
struck down Bonnivet, the French commander, and
Bayard, the last representative of mediaeval chivalry.
The death of Bayard indeed aptly symbolizes the
change from the old military order to the new.

The battle of the Sesia, even more than Bicocca,
was a victory for the arquebus and the musket. At
Bicocca the firearms had been for the most part
stationed behind earthworks and hedged round with
pikes: at the Sesia they were manoeuvred independently in the open field. For the first time in an
important engagement the pikeman appeared as an
auxiliary to the arquebusier. The missile weapons
shaped the course of the fight; the weapons of shock
conformed to the action of the missile weapons, protected them in defence, supported them in attack.
This combination of arms is henceforth the rule in
the imperial army. At Pavia the marquis of Pescara
showed perfect mastery of his instrument. Spanish

arquebusiers and musketeers, supported by pikemen and cavalry to protect them against hostile men-at-arms, scattered on the flanks and rear of the massed horse and foot of the enemy, broke their formation by steady shooting, withdrew before them when they charged, and finally, when they were thoroughly demoralized, advanced to close quarters, still in conjunction with pikemen and cavalry, and won the most decisive victory of that generation[1]. We find the same skilful combination of missile weapons with the arme blanche in the fighting of the Tuscan Black Band round Naples in 1528[2], and again on the imperial side at the battle of Landriano[3], which finally expelled the French from Italy.

During these later Italian campaigns the activities of the arquebusier were very varied. Both in siege warfare and in open fighting he was the subject of ceaseless experiment. Covering fire from arquebuses was employed, as we have seen, at Brescia in 1512 for the purpose of protecting the advance of the storming party. It was employed in the same year by the Spanish and Papal army at Bologna to facilitate the placing of the siege artillery[4]. It was employed

---

[1] See Du Bellay, *Mémoires*, bk. II; Giovio, *Vita Marchionis Piscariae*, bk. VI.

[2] Giovio, *Istorie*, bk. XXV. The Black Band numbered at this time about 3000, of whom the majority were arquebusiers (Varchi, *Storia Fiorentina*, ed. Milanesi, bk. IV, § 28). Their opponents at Naples were equally addicted to the new tactics; cf. Segni (*Storie Fiorentine*, bk. II): "facevano gl' imperiali ogni notte uscir fuori parte della cavalleria mescolata cogli archibusieri, per condurre vettovaglie e tener qualche strada aperta." [3] Du Bellay, bk. III, p. 102.

[4] Coccinius, *De bellis italicis*, p. 201.

at Milan in 1521 to assist in the kidnapping of a
sleepy French sentinel from whom much important
information was subsequently extracted. It was employed by Pescara in the same year to aid an assault
on Como, and again in 1524 at Meltio to support a raid
by pikemen. When he was in a position to take the
enemy by surprise, as at Milan in 1521 and Lodi in 1522,
Pescara even used arquebusiers as storming troops[1].

It is recorded of Gian Paolo Vitelli, who died in
1499, that he was in the habit of plucking out the
eyes and cutting off the hands of arquebusiers captured in battle, because he deemed it disgraceful that
noble men-at-arms should be shot from a distance
by low-born infantrymen[2]. Twenty-nine years after
the death of Vitelli the people of Florence, in whose
service he had fought his last campaigns, revived
their long extinct militia by a law which laid down
in a special clause that care should be taken to raise
as many arquebusiers as possible[3]. These two facts
placed thus in juxtaposition illustrate very effectively

[1] For these various operations see Giovio, *Vita Marchionis
Piscariae*. It is worth noting in this connexion that arquebuses
were used with great effect by both sides in the naval action
between Filippino Doria and the imperialists in the Gulf of
Salerno in 1528 (Guicciardini, *Istoria d' Italia*, bk. XIX).

[2] Giovio, *Elogi*, bk. IV. Vitelli seems to have entertained
similar feelings against gunners: according to Nardi (*Istorie
della città di Firenze*, bk. II, § 6), after capturing the castello
of Buti in 1498 he cut off the hands of all the gunners of the
garrison.

[3] *Provisione della Milizia e Ordinanza del Popolo Fiorentino*,
6 Nov. 1528. In the earlier militia of 1499–1512 those men
who did not carry pikes were left free to choose a balestra or
a schioppetto or a roncola or a spiede grande (Machiavelli,
Legazione XIX, doc. 4), which shows that no special impor-

the change which the Italian wars directly produced in the character of the infantry arm. In 1494 there were two distinct categories of infantry. There were the highly trained massed pikemen, swordsmen and halberdiers, and there were the despised, ill-disciplined arquebusiers and crossbowmen. The Italian wars welded these two classes into one. After a period of competition between them it became clear that each was necessary to complete the efficiency of the other. Those who carried missile weapons inflicted greater losses on the enemy, were more mobile and less affected by difficulties of ground, but they needed the pike to stiffen them against cavalry, and to break by shock action the enemy who had been weakened by musketry fire. In the Swiss army at the end of the fifteenth century the arquebusier was auxiliary to the pikeman; at the Sesia and at Pavia the pikeman went into action as a support to the arquebusier. This change in the relative importance of the two weapons is a measure of the influence of the Italian campaigns on infantry tactics. The pike, however, though ceasing to be the paramount weapon, remained as essential to infantry organization as the firearm. Indeed, as the only trustworthy weapon for wet weather[1], and as the weapon for ultimate action

tance was then attached to small arms. In 1528, of the 3000 men raised, 1700 were arquebusiers, 1000 pikemen, and 300 carried miscellaneous weapons (Varchi, *Storia Fiorentina*, bk. VIII, § 7).

[1] Heavy rain sometimes prevented the ignition of the charge, *e.g.* at the defence of Brescia 1512 (Mocenico, *La guerra di Cambrai*, bk. IV), and at St Angelo in 1529 (Guicciardini, *Istoria d' Italia*, bk. XIX).

at all times, it continued to be the more indispensable of the two. But we must picture the two weapons henceforth not as rivals but as allies. Infantry assumes a dual nature: within its formations pike-men and musketeers are held together in mutual dependence and mutual support. This type of infantry, adopted first by the national armies which fought in Italy, became common to the whole of Europe, and remained so till at the end of the seventeenth century the invention of the bayonet united the advantages of missile and shock weapons in the hands of the in-dividual soldier.

Besides fostering and popularizing a new type of infantry, the Italian wars continued the process of raising the status of the footsoldier. The military leaders of Europe had been astonished by the report of the early victories of the Swiss: when they saw the Swiss at close quarters in Italy they were hardly less impressed by their martial bearing. Their machine-like drill, their march discipline, and their air of com-parative refinement reminded scholars of the soldiers of antiquity, and helped captains to realize that a company of infantry was not necessarily a motley rout of straggling crossbowmen[1]. There are many

[1] Cf. Landucci's description of the new Florentine militia (*Diario*, 15 Feb. 1505): "fece la mostra in Piazza 400 fanti, i quali aveva ordinati el Gonfaloniere, di nostri contadini, e dava loro a ogniuno un farsetto bianco, un paio di calze alla divisa, bianche e rosse, e una berretta bianca, e le scarpette, e un petto di ferro e le lance, e a chi scioppietti....E così fu tenuto la più bella cosa che si ordinassi mai per la città di Firenze." A similar note of admiration is perceptible in Giovio's description of the Swiss marching through Rome in 1495

indications of this change of spirit. Uniformity of dress begins to appear—sometimes as a mere distinguishing badge, at other times as a resplendent livery[1]. In the French army, in which, more than in any other, the prestige of the cavalry was maintained, renowned captains[2]—nay, the king himself[3]—were not ashamed to command unmounted troops. At Ravenna the Spanish foot were considered the mainstay of their side and for their benefit the men-at-arms were deliberately sacrificed. From this time onward modern Europe, like the ancient world, recognizes the true military importance of infantry. This does not mean that the footsoldier was ever held actually in higher esteem than his more specialized fellow-combatants. On the contrary, even in the armies of to-day the infantry remains somewhat of a Cinderella among the arms. But it is no longer forgotten that Cinderella was more useful than her sisters.

(*Istorie*, bk. II), in Benedetti's description of the drill of the Germans in the Italian camp before Novara in the same year (*Il fatto d' arme del Tarro*, bk. II), and in Giustinian's remarks on Cesare Borgia's infantry at Rome in 1503 (*Dispaccio* 360).

[1] *E.g.* at Ravenna the French wore white crosses, the Spaniards coloured ones (see *Relacion de los sucesos de las armas de España*, in *Colec. de doc. ined.* vol. LXXIX).

[2] *E.g.* Bayard in 1509 (Loyal Serviteur, ch. XXIX).

[3] At Marignano (Du Bellay, *Mémoires*, bk. I; Giovio, *Istorie*, bk. XV).

NOTE

An instructive index to the increased use of small fire-arms in the course of the Italian wars is furnished by a comparison of the casualties due to arquebus fire among prominent military commanders before and after the peace of Noyon, 1516.

Only three instances of such casualties occur before that date, viz.,

Pitigliano	at Novara	in 1495
Nemours	Cerignola	1503
Marcantonio Colonna	Verona	1516

After 1516 we find the following instances:

Lorenzo de' Medici	at Mondolfo	in 1517
Bonnivet	the Sesia	1524
Bayard	the Sesia	1524
Giovanni de' Medici	Pavia	1525
Palisse	Pavia	1525
Tremoille	Pavia	1525
Lescun	Pavia	1525
Bourbon	Rome	1527
Orange	Florence	1530

CHAPTER IV

CAVALRY

IN the first of the series of French armies which invaded Italy between 1494 and 1528 the cavalry amounted to about two-thirds of the whole[1]: in the last the proportion was one-eleventh[2]. In the case of the Spanish army, which began to reduce its proportion of cavalry before 1494[3], the acceleration of that process during the Italian wars is hardly less striking. On the Garigliano the proportion was one cavalryman to five infantrymen[4]; at Pavia it was one cavalryman to twelve infantrymen[5]. Machiavelli, writing in 1520, argues that the foot should be twenty times as numerous as the horse[6]. This rapid alteration in the accepted ratio between infantry and cavalry would lead one to infer that the Italian wars produced a partial eclipse of the cavalry arm by the infantry. The depreciation of the mounted soldier in which Machiavelli and other writers of the period indulge might also seem to warrant such a generalization[7]. There are other facts, however, which point

[1] This proportion is accepted by Duparcq, *L'art de la guerre*, vol. II, p. 26, and the *Cambridge Modern History*, vol. I, ch. IV.

[2] Du Bellay, *Mémoires*, bk. III, p. 86.

[3] Jähns, *Handbuch*, pp. 1044 *seq.*

[4] Guicciardini, *Istoria d' Italia*, bk. VI, followed by Rüstow, *Geschichte der Infanterie*, vol. I, p. 276.

[5] Guicciardini, *Istoria d' Italia*, bk. XVI.

[6] *Arte della guerra*, bk. II.

[7] *E.g.* Machiavelli, *loc. cit.*; Giovio, *Istorie*, bk. IV, p. 101.

to a different conclusion. Heavy cavalry continued
to prove itself unequalled for shock tactics. It is true
that massed pikemen and entrenchments were an
effective defence against such tactics, but they were
not a substitute for them. No other troops could
develop the driving power of a squadron of charging
men-at-arms. Consequently the man-at-arms remained essential in every battle, and in at least one
first-class action he decided the issue[1]. Again, the
man-at-arms continued to be surrounded by his
mediaeval prestige. He was still usually of gentle
birth. A vague inherited freemasonry, which united
him in spirit more closely to the men-at-arms of other
armies than to the infantry of his own side, gave to
his peculiar status an international recognition[2].
Further, and most important of all, a new type of
cavalry now for the first time emerges as a separate
organization. As the Italian wars proceeded lightly
armed horsemen, such as those which formed part
of the French "lances[3]," were collected into special
formations and allotted special duties. Giovanni de'
Medici defined these duties thus: to protect the remainder of the army, to assure the food supply, to
observe, to bring back intelligence, and to keep the
enemy in suspense[4]. An arm which, during a generation of intense warfare, not only maintained its high

[1] At Marignano, according to Francis I (Letter to the
duchesse d'Angoulesme).
[2] Cf. the relations between the French and Spanish men-
at-arms during the siege of Barletta 1502–3 (see Loyal Serviteur, *Histoire de Bayart*, ch. XXIII), and before the battle of
Ravenna (*ibid*. ch. LIV).   [3] See p. 3 above.
[4] Rossi, *Vita di Giovanni de' Medici*, p. 244.

reputation but also developed new activities cannot be said to have suffered a decline. It is true that the infantry outstripped the cavalry in the general advance towards greater efficiency, and that consequently the cavalry found itself in the end filling a subordinate rôle. This loss of standing, however, was purely relative. For horse as well as foot it is actually a period of continuous progress. The mounted arm no doubt develops more slowly and has finally to recognize its own limitations. But that in itself is progress.

There was a broad resemblance between the men-at-arms of all European countries, but the highest reputation was deservedly enjoyed by those of the French army. They were a royal cavalry, directly subject to the king and paid by him. A keen rivalry for promotion, which depended chiefly on valour, maintained a high standard of efficiency. They were, almost without exception, the sons of noble houses. Consequently they could afford to equip themselves well. They carried a heavy lance, an iron mace, and elaborate armour. Their horses were big and strong and wore armour also. They exceeded the heavy cavalry of other nations in numbers and in discipline[1]. Their characteristic tactics were furious charges in compact bodies of 400[2] or 500[3]. The Italian men-at-

[1] Giovio, *Istorie*, bks. II and XV, p. 346; Guicciardini, *Istoria d' Italia*, bk. I; and cf. *Relazioni of the Venetian Ambassadors*, Series I, vol. VI, p. 14.

[2] As at Seminara (Giovio, *Vita Consalvi Cordubae*, bk. I).

[3] As at Marignano (Letter of Francis I to the duchesse d'Angoulesme).

arms, as we should expect in a country which had long cultivated cavalry at the expense of infantry, were likewise highly trained and well armed. They seem to have carried a longer lance than the French, and to have preferred the axe to the mace[1]. Organized for battle they were less effective than the French, but as individual combatants they were nowise inferior. In Italy was first undertaken the scientific breeding of war horses. For this purpose Giovan Francesco Gonzaga, marquis of Mantua, who commanded the Italian army at Fornovo, imported stallions from Turkey, from Spain, and from Ireland[2]. Throughout the period we are considering the cavalry of France and of the Italian states continued to excel that of the other belligerents. The mounted troops of Germany carried little body-armour and were but lightly equipped. They rode horses which were clumsy and entirely unprotected[3]. In battle they did not co-operate with other arms[4]. The emperor Maximilian, who was alive to the defects of his cavalry, made no attempt to improve it, but chose rather to organize new formations on the French model[5]. As to the Spanish men-at-arms, inferior equipment made them the least formidable heavy cavalry in Europe. Their helmets and shields were

[1] Giovio, *Vita Consalvi Cordubae*, bk. II; Benedetti, *Il fatto d' arme del Tarro*, bk. I, p. 24.

[2] Giovio, *Elogi*, bk. V.

[3] Machiavelli, *Ritratti delle cose della Magna* (*Opere*, vol. VI, p. 324).

[4] *Relazioni of the Venetian Ambassadors*, Series I, vol. VI, pp. 14 *seq*.

[5] Porto, *Lettere Storiche*, no. 35.

often of leather; their lances were so light as to be negligible against the French and Italians; their discipline, moreover, unlike that of the Spanish infantry, was not equal to supplementing the defects of their arms[1].

During the Italian wars there was no important development or modification in the employment of heavy cavalry. Men-at-arms were the shock troops par excellence and were used on all occasions when the maximum impetus was needed in an assault. When used skilfully, when, that is to say, their charges were prepared for and supported by other arms, they were able, as at Marignano, to prevail against the formidable pikes of the Swiss. When, on the other hand, their work was not co-ordinated with that of the infantry and the artillery, they proved unable of themselves to achieve victory. The battle of the Sesia, which proclaimed so many valuable lessons to those who had ears to hear, showed the superiority of cavalry and infantry acting together over cavalry and infantry acting separately. First the French men-at-arms and then the Swiss pikemen tried to repel the mixed force of horse and foot which was pressing in upon them, and in each case the attempt was broken with heavy loss[2]. At Pavia the same lesson was taught with yet greater cogency. Even a non-military, non-European, and unofficial writer who was not present at the action recognized that the victory on that day was due to skilful co-

---

[1] Giovio, *Istorie*, bk. III: *Vita Consalvi Cordubae*, bk. I.
[2] Giovio, *Vita Marchionis Piscariae*, bk. III.

operation between mounted and unmounted troops[1]. Francis I, however, in his conversation after the battle, failed to realize, or at any rate to admit, so obvious a truth[2]. This inability either to learn or to unlearn, which recalls the political attitude of his Bourbon descendants, undoubtedly accounts for his final failure to establish his power in Italy.

Only two further remarks need be made upon the tactical employment of men-at-arms in the Italian wars. In the first place it should be noted that their vulnerability lay in their horses. This had been recognized in the Middle Ages. The English archers learned during the Hundred Years' War that an arrow which seldom drew blood when launched against a mailed knight usually produced a prisoner and a ransom when it disabled his mount. Horse-armour, which was adopted to meet this danger, remained in use, as we have seen, among the French and Italian men-at-arms who fought in Italy. Against the pike it was a useful protection, but with the spread of small firearms the problem became once more acute and remained insoluble. Monluc during the campaign of 1521–2 had no fewer than five horses killed beneath him[3]. Though the high mortality among horses cannot be said to have had any direct influence on the relative decline of the heavy cavalry, it certainly furnished a reason for developing a more mobile mounted force which should offer a less favour-

[1] Joseph ben Joshua ben Meir, *Chronicles*, para. 650.

[2] Giovio, *Vita Marchionis Piscariae*, bk. VI; Rossi, *Vita di Giovanni de' Medici*.

[3] Monluc, *Mémoires*, bk. I.

able target to the enemy. The second point to be noticed about the man-at-arms is his adaptability. The old practice was continued of using him at times as a footsoldier. In that condition his heavy armour unfitted him for any operations which required quick movement, but enabled him on the other hand to run greater risks than the comparatively unprotected infantryman.. He was therefore especially useful in the intense but restricted fighting by which an entrance was forced into a besieged town. Dismounted men-at-arms acted as storming troops in most of the more famous sieges of the Italian wars—notably at Padua in 1509[1], at Brescia in 1512[2], at Milan in 1526[3], and at Pavia in 1528[4]. Another side to the activities of the men-at-arms was their occasional performance of the duties of light cavalry. In the Venetian campaign of 1514 men-at-arms escorted the supplies and guarded the communications of the Spanish army[5]. French men-at-arms were the soul of the most brilliant raid of that age—the spearhead of the swift thrust from the Alps in 1515 which surprised Prospero Colonna at Villafranca[6]. A long silent gallop into the enemy's country, the rushing of a town-gate, and the capture of a hostile commander while he is unsuspectingly sitting at table—a feat so daring has seldom been performed even by the light cavalry

[1] Loyal Serviteur, *Histoire de Bayart*, ch. XXXIII.
[2] Porto, *Lettere Storiche*, no. 65.
[3] Guicciardini, *Istoria d' Italia*, bk. XVII.
[4] *Ibid.* bk. XIX.
[5] *Ibid.* bk. XI.
[6] Loyal Serviteur, *Histoire de Bayart*, ch. LIX.

whose business it is to do such things[1]. No estimate
of the men-at-arms of this period would be just which
did not recognize their versatility. Their willingness
to undertake the most unpromising tasks contrasts
very favourably with the complaining spirit in which
an appeal for a special effort was often met by the
infantry. The French men-at-arms in particular were
well-disciplined and many-sided. By the irony of
fate this very excellence of theirs wrought the destruction of the cause for which they bled. At
Marignano their valour deceived King Francis into
regarding them as his principal arm[2]. At Pavia he
acted on this misconception[3] and was led captive by
his enemies.

The Spanish men-at-arms who served under the
marquis of Pescara are said to have been depressed
and discontented because he relied unduly on infantry
and light cavalry[4]. The historian who records this
fact remarks that in depending chiefly on infantry
and light cavalry the marquis of Pescara was merely
following the teaching of the ancients. It is doubtful

[1] The importance of this raid was not merely spectacular;
cf. Mocenico's words (*La guerra di Cambrai*, bk. VI): "e fu
grandissimo danno a gli Suizzeri, perche non haveano altri
cavallieri, che gli potessero ministrare le vettovaglie." Champier points out (*Les Gestes de Bayard*, bk. III, ch. I) that
Prospero Colonna relied for security on the obstacle of the Po:
the fording of this was not the least brilliant feature of the
raid.

[2] Cf. his letter to the duchesse d'Angoulesme, written after
the battle.

[3] Cf. Giovio's description of the battle in *Vita Marchionis
Piscariae*, bk. VI.

[4] Giovio, *loc. cit.* bk. V.

whether Pescara, who was not deeply versed in the humanities, realized that his military method had the sanction of antiquity. It is certain, however, that his practice of the art of war met the needs of his time. His development of the infantry arm has already been discussed. He was less instrumental in the development of light cavalry, but the use he made of it in gaining his victories marks its definite arrival as an independent arm[1]. Although light cavalry had long figured in Western armies, it had not yet generally achieved an existence separate from that of the heavy cavalry; the Italian wars brought it to birth as a distinct formation, and under the fostering care of the marquis of Pescara and of Giovanni de' Medici it soon filled an honourable position in the military economy of Europe.

Light horsemen existed originally as auxiliaries to the men-at-arms. By 1494 they had attained a separate standing in Spain[2], but elsewhere they were still grouped with the heavy cavalry. Among the French and the Italians each man-at-arms had from four to six light horsemen attached to him in the unit known as the "lance[3]." In the early years of

[1] It is noteworthy that Pescara's earliest command was that of the light cavalry in the army of the League at the battle of Ravenna.

[2] Jähns, *Handbuch*, pp. 1067 *seq.*

[3] Seyssel, *La victoire...*[à]...*Aignadel* (in Godefroy, *Histoire de Louis XII*, p. 131); *Relazioni of the Venetian Ambassadors*, Series II, vol. V, p. 301. Two mounted bowmen (the usual type of light horsemen at this time) were commonly reckoned the military equivalent of a man-at-arms (cf. Bembo, *Istoria Viniziana*, bk. IV, p. 177), though in an agreement between Ferdinand of Aragon and Venice (*ibid.* bk. III, p. 117) the

the Italian wars the lance was a unit not only for organization but also for tactics. At Fornovo[1] and at Seminara[2] light and heavy cavalry charged together in mixed formations. Gradually, however, as commanders began to see the advantage of using the more mobile horsemen as a separate arm for special functions, the lance system lost its tactical significance and light cavalry became the subject of experiment. Its distinctive weapons hitherto had been the light lance and, more especially, the bow. With the extension of the use of firearms came the gradual adoption of the arquebus. The first commander to employ mounted arquebusiers was Camillo Vitelli[3]. As early as 1495 this condottiere had justified his faith in light cavalry when at the battle of Lucera he routed a large formation of German pikemen by the skilful manoeuvring of a force of mounted archers[4]. He introduced a new element into European warfare by the success of his experiments with mounted arquebusiers. The practice of arming light cavalry with firearms soon spread over Italy and into France[5]. Fifty mounted arquebusiers were serving under Cesare Borgia and 300 under Vitellozzo Vitelli in

Venetian man-at-arms is considered only one and a half times as valuable as the Venetian light horseman, perhaps because the light horse in question were stradiots (concerning whom see p. 72 below).

[1] Commines, *Mémoires*, bk. VIII, ch. VI.

[2] Giovio, *Vita Consalvi Cordubae*, bk. I.

[3] Giovio, *Elogi*, bk. IV.   [4] *Ibid.*

[5] Mounted arquebusiers figure in the army of the duke of Milan as early as 1494 (Sanuto, *La spedizione di Carlo VIII*, bk. I, pp. 75, 78). We find Venice using them in the Pisan war in 1497 (Bembo, *Istoria Viniziana*, bk. IV, p. 159).

1502[1]. In 1510 we find Luigi Porto, a captain of light cavalry in the Venetian service, arming a part of his company with firearms and using them with great success against the German cavalry in Friuli[2]. Only one-tenth of the light cavalry raised by Florence in 1511 carried lances; the remainder were allowed to use crossbows or arquebuses according to their inclination[3]. In the Swiss army of invasion of 1511— a force we have already noticed for the high proportion of arquebusiers among the infantry—firearms were carried by no less than half the mounted troops[4]. Even Machiavelli, who was never convinced of the supreme importance of firearms, admits the necessity of having a part of the cavalry so armed[5]. Nevertheless, in spite of this rapid extension of the use of firearms among the cavalry, the crossbow remained all through the Italian wars their chief missile weapon. The main reason for this was the unwieldiness of the arquebus in the hands of a mounted soldier. Until the Germans invented a lighter weapon (Faustrohr, pistola) during the Schmalkaldic War the mounted archer was preserved from extinction by his superior mobility[6]. Another reason was the introduction into Italy of a new type of light horse which achieved such marked success without the aid of missile weapons that, during the last phase of the wars,

[1] Machiavelli, *Legazione XI*, docs. 44, 85.
[2] Porto, *Lettere Storiche*, no. 47.
[3] Canestrini, *Scritti inediti di Machiavelli*, pp. xlvi and 377 *seq*.
[4] Guicciardini, *Istoria d' Italia*, bk. IX.
[5] *Arte della guerra*, bk. II.   [6] Jähns, *Handbuch*, Vorblick.

cavalry commanders ceased to interest themselves in the rival claims of crossbow and arquebus.

This new light cavalry became famous under the name of the stradiots. The stradiots were recruited by the Venetian government among the peoples of the Balkans. They rode swift Turkish horses and carried a light lance, a sword, a shield, and a breast-plate[1]. Prolonged warfare against the Turk had given them a ferocity in battle and a capacity for enduring hardships unequalled by any Western troops[2]. The prospect of plunder made them eager to undertake service in Italy[3]. When they first came in contact with the French in the skirmishing before the battle of Fornovo their tactics showed them to be a true light cavalry. By repeated charges and retirements they lured the enemy to pursue; when the pursuit had sufficiently disintegrated his formation they turned upon his isolated groups of men-at-arms and cut them to pieces[4]. So successful were these tactics against the French cavalry that in the march to Asti after Fornovo Charles VIII was obliged to defend his rearguard with German infantry well supplied with arquebuses and artillery[5]. From this time onward the number of stradiots serving in Italy increased

[1] Benedetti, *Il fatto d' arme del Tarro*, bk. II.

[2] Commines, *Mémoires*, bk. VIII, ch. V. Such was their ferocity that in 1498, during the Pisan war, Florence decreed that all stradiots who were taken prisoner should be killed (Bembo, *Istoria Viniziana*, bk. IV, p. 165).

[3] Priuli, *De bello gallico*, col. 32 (in Muratori, *Rer. It. Script.* vol. XXIV, where the work is attributed to Sanuto).

[4] Giovio, *Istorie*, bk. II.

[5] Commines, *Mémoires*, bk. VIII, ch. VII.

continuously, first as part of the Venetian army, and later as independent mercenaries[1]. They tended to discard the shield in favour of the helmet and cuirass, and to adopt the mace in place of the lance as their principal weapon. So armed they are said to have achieved a marked ascendancy over the French men-at-arms in the skirmishing round Verona in 1516[2]. Among the stradiots who served under Lautrec in 1527–8 the earlier and the later styles of equipment were represented about equally[3].

With the example of the Venetian stradiots before them, the commanders of other armies began to pay more attention to the training of light cavalry for independent action[4]. The Spaniards, who had already made some progress in this direction, continued to exploit the tactical advantage which it gave them over the French. Light cavalry were of particular assistance to Gonsalvo de Cordova in his Neapolitan campaigns; their activity during the siege of Atella cut all the land communications of the garrison and forced it to surrender before succour could arrive by sea; their successful screening of Gonsalvo's move-

[1] Stradiots served on both sides in the war between Louis XII and Ludovico Sforza in 1499 (D'Auton, *Conqueste de Milan*) and in the Garigliano campaign (D'Auton, *Chroniques de Louis XII*, 1503, ch. XXI; Bembo, *Istoria Viniziana*, bk. III). They also formed part of Alviano's force defeated by the Florentines at the Torre di San Vincenzo in 1505 (Nardi, *Istorie della città di Firenze*, bk. IV, § 101).

[2] Giovio, *Istorie*, bk. XVIII.   [3] *Ibid.* bk. XXV.

[4] *E.g.* at the battle at the Torre di San Vincenzo in 1505 the Florentine light horse were separated from the men-at-arms when they went into action (Nardi, *Istorie della città di Firenze*, bk. IV, § 101).

ments before Cerignola gave him freedom to make
the dispositions which brought victory; while their
part in the pursuit from the Garigliano was a deciding factor in the operations which won Naples for
Spain[1]. In the war against the League of Cambrai
the stradiots provide the only bright spot in the
disastrous campaigns of the Venetian armies. In
1509 they interfered so seriously with Louis XII's
communications that they forced him to seek battle
at all costs[2]; when that battle had broken the army
of the republic they continued to hang on the flanks
and rear of the victor, to cut off consignments of
supplies, and, with the help of information supplied
by the peasantry, to make successful raids against
isolated parties of the enemy[3]. By one of these raids,
undertaken in the blackest period of the war and
resulting in the capture of no less a personage than
the marquis of Mantua, they were able to raise considerably the moral of their side. The value of their
extreme mobility was again strikingly shown when
in the winter of 1511, by galloping all the way from
Stellata to Bologna, a party of them was able to
stiffen the attitude of Julius II in his negotiations with
Chaumont[4]. It should be noted, however, that all these
activities of the best light cavalry of the day were of
an auxiliary character. They did not change or decide
the course of a campaign. Although Venice had an
almost unlimited supply of these splendid troops, she

[1] Guicciardini, *Istoria d' Italia*, bks. III and V *passim*.
[2] Porto, *Lettere Storiche*, no. 12.
[3] Guicciardini, *Istoria d' Italia*, bk. IX.
[4] *Ibid.*; Buonaccorsi, *Diario*, p. 153.

was not able by their means to neutralize the inferiority of her other arms, or to prevent the barbarian from devastating for seven years her fairest provinces. When in 1514 the Spanish army advanced almost to the gates of the capital Bartolommeo d' Alviano, the commander of the Venetian forces, relying on the superior numbers of his infantry and the better quality of his cavalry, attempted to cut off the enemy's retreat. His measures were admirably conceived and ably carried out, but, when the time came for dealing a decisive blow at the trapped Spaniards, the Italian infantry fled at the first encounter and the enemy escaped[1]. The lessons of the Venetian war were not lost on the belligerents. They recognized, though in varying degrees, that cavalry, however excellent, could achieve little unless used in conjunction with an effective infantry. Cavalry, in other words, was a secondary arm. Thus side by side with the actual progress in cavalry tactics inaugurated by the stradiots there occurred that relative decline in the importance of cavalry which has already been noted as characteristic of the period[2].

The history of the light cavalry arm during the last decade of the Italian wars does not show any new developments. There is merely an accentuation of earlier tendencies. The separation of the light horse-

[1] Guicciardini, *Istoria d' Italia*, bk. XI.
[2] Cf. the military policy of the Florentine government in these years. A native infantry began to be raised in 1499: a native cavalry was not raised till 1511–12—and then it consisted of light cavalry only (see Machiavelli, *Opere*, vol. VI, p. 352).

man from the man-at-arms is completed, and it is generally realized that he has special duties of observation, protection, skirmishing, raiding, and pursuit. Shock tactics are left to the heavy cavalry. The marquis of Pescara used light cavalry at the Sesia and at Pavia to protect and support his arquebusiers: when the skirmishing tactics of these troops had had sufficient effect his men-at-arms charged and broke the enemy[1]. The most famous *corps d'élite* of the closing campaigns, Giovanni de' Medici's Black Band, was composed of light infantry and light cavalry. Later, as we have seen[2], a force of mounted infantry was added. The discipline and efficiency of the Black Band and the competition among commanders to secure its services bear witness to the progress which had been made in specialization since the days of the lance system[3].

Specialization is indeed the word which best describes the development of the art of war at this period. The functions of the infantry and of the cavalry are subdivided. A light infantry is evolved side by side with the pikemen. A light cavalry separates itself for special duties from the men-at-arms. In the same way the special provinces of infantry and cavalry become more sharply differentiated. The overlapping of functions within the army —an inheritance from the Middle Ages—is gradually corrected. Retribution follows the employment of

---

[1] Giovio, *Vita Marchionis Piscariae*, bk. III.
[2] p. 53 above.
[3] See Rossi, *Vita di Giovanni de' Medici*.

cavalry for work which can be better done by infantry. In the long run those commanders are victorious who realize most clearly the limitations of the cavalry arm. This same truth was stated in a different way in connexion with the infantry. Then it was shown how the imperial army, guided by the marquis of Pescara's strategic sense and his instinct for exploiting the capabilities of the infantry, eventually drove the French from the peninsula. We are now in a position to consider briefly the reverse side of the process, and to see how the French disasters followed a too great reliance on the cavalry arm.

Machiavelli recognizes three disadvantages in cavalry as compared with infantry: it is hampered by difficult country, it is less easily manoeuvred, and it is harder to rally[1]. It is to the interest of a commander who is superior in cavalry to bring his opponent to battle under conditions which tend to minimize these disadvantages. If he can force the enemy into flat country where his cavalry has freedom to manoeuvre, and if his cavalry is numerous and well disciplined, he stands a reasonable chance of gaining the victory. Several times during the Italian wars the French, who were continuously superior in cavalry, defeated their opponents by methods of this kind. When, however, the greater military skill of the enemy forced them to fight in circumstances unfavourable to cavalry they were invariably conquered. At the battle of Fornovo both sides placed their chief reliance on cavalry, and the French were

[1] *Arte della guerra*, bk. II.

able to repulse the Italians because the marquis of Mantua, despite his reputation as a leader of mounted troops, launched his attack across a river-bed and up a steep bank covered with vegetation[1]. Agnadello, on the other hand, is an example of the successful manoeuvring of an enemy on to ground where he could be made to suffer the consequences of his inferiority in cavalry. The Venetian army took up an inaccessible position and refused battle. King Louis by his march on Rivolta forced them to follow him. For four miles they were able to retain their advantage of position, but as soon as the country became less difficult the French attacked[2]. The issue was doubtful until the French men-at-arms succeeded in extending the fight to the open country[3]. Then the Venetian rearguard was broken by the most dreaded shock troops in Christendom, and the remainder of the army retreated in disorder.

Each of the four decisive battles of Ravenna, Marignano, Bicocca, and Pavia took the form of an attack on an entrenched camp. The presence of entrenchments on a field of battle cripples cavalry. Consequently the cavalry leader must either compel a change of terrain or content himself with playing a subsidiary rôle. Ravenna is a classic instance of the first course. The plan of the Spanish and Papal com-

---

[1] Benedetti, *Il fatto d' arme del Tarro*, bk. I; Giovio, *Istorie*, bk. II.

[2] Prato, *De rebus mediolanensibus*, pp. 272 *seq.* (in *Arch. Stor. It.*, vol. III).

[3] Marillac, *Vie du connétable de Bourbon*; Guicciardini, *Istoria d' Italia*, bk. VIII.

manders—to keep behind their defences and to await attack—was fully justified by the fact that their chief strength lay in their infantry. Their defences, however, were not proof against the French artillery. A devastating bombardment at last forced their cavalry into the open; there they were outfought and routed by the French men-at-arms; the Spanish infantry advanced to their assistance, was subjected by the French to a combined attack of all arms, and compelled to abandon the field. At Bicocca the French again attacked an entrenched camp, but this time they wasted their cavalry in a suicidal attempt to force an entrance. Instead of keeping the cavalry in reserve, as at Ravenna, until the enemy had been expelled from his camp by other means, they launched it against a defensive system which even the infantry were unable to carry. At Marignano and at Pavia it was the French who were entrenched. In neither case, therefore, were they able to use their cavalry to full advantage. In the former action the Swiss infantry succumbed to a combined attack by infantry, cavalry, and artillery: it was the co-operation of all arms, and not the preponderance of one, which decided the day in favour of the French. At Pavia, where similar tactics might have produced similar results, King Francis, in his eagerness to bring his cavalry into action, masked his own guns[1] and lost touch with his infantry[2]. The French men-at-arms,

---

[1] Du Bellay, *Mémoires*, bk. II; Giovio, *Vita Marchionis Piscariae*, bk. VI.

[2] Giovio, *loc. cit.*

thus isolated, were helpless against the carefully correlated offensive tactics in which the imperial horse and foot had been trained by the marquis of Pescara. The Spanish infantry atoned for its defeat at Ravenna by the annihilation of the French cavalry and the capture of the French king.

It must not be supposed, however, that at Pavia the tactical lessons of Ravenna were reversed. From the point of view of military progress the one battle was not the reversal but the fulfilment of the other. At the earlier battle the French won because they combined their different arms more successfully than their opponents. At the later battle the imperialists won because they combined their arms even more intimately and more aptly. Gaston de Foix was victorious because he withheld his men-at-arms till the fight reached a stage favourable to their employment, but he lost his life in the end because he led some of them into a position where cavalry could not succeed[1]. There was at Ravenna another young commander, with a frail body and an eye of fire, who led the light cavalry of Spain in an unsupported charge and paid for his blunder by falling into the enemy's hands. He saw the Spanish infantry retire from the field for lack of such support as his own cavalry, properly handled, could easily have given, and his subsequent history proves that he was quick to read the meaning of the catastrophe. He was the marquis of Pescara.

[1] Loyal Serviteur, *Histoire de Bayart*, ch. LIV; *Relacion de los sucesos de las armas de España* 1511–12.

CHAPTER V

ARTILLERY

IN the matter of artillery the Italian wars of the Renaissance period were characterized not by new inventions but by the classification and development of existing types. Already at the end of the fifteenth century the armies of Europe were familiar with the numerous varieties of gun with which the Italian campaigns were fought. Martini, writing a few years before Charles VIII's expedition, describes ten different types of gun and adds that his list is by no means exhaustive[1]. It is noticeable, however, that he draws no distinction between artillery and small arms. The bombarda, twenty feet long and firing a ball of 300 pounds weight, is catalogued with the scoppietto, from two to three feet long and firing shot weighing a fraction of an ounce[2]. Neither does he make the modern separation between field artillery and siege artillery. All firearms are classed as artillery. He does not investigate the reasons for the existence of guns of different sizes: he is preoccupied with the fact that they employ the common medium of gunpowder. Gunpowder is still sufficiently awe-inspiring to dominate the military imagination and to hinder the process of sober experiment and methodical

[1] *Trattato di architettura civile e militare*, bk. v, ch. i.
[2] 4 to 6 dramme.

tabulation of results by which alone artillery can be progressively improved. The mystery which surrounded the origin of this monstrous birth of the Middle Ages continued to cling to it for two centuries. The practice of gunnery was the jealously kept secret of an exclusive craft. The enlightened Guicciardini can describe artillery as a pest[1]. Even Machiavelli, who, characteristically, pokes fun at the claims made on behalf of gunpowder, is forced to admit the important moral effect of the fear which it inspires[2]. Both these public men, however, lived to see, if not to recognize, the beginning of the change from the mediaeval to the modern view of artillery. This change from the mysterious to the scientific, from ritual to empiricism, is represented in a military treatise published by Niccolò Tartaglia in 1538. Tartaglia excludes the subject of hand firearms from his discussion of gunnery, but deals on the other hand in great detail with such questions as sighting, trajectories and ballistics[3]. It is the practical background of this theoretical development which we have to consider in the present chapter.

The division between siege guns and field guns occurred earlier than that between artillery and small arms. From the first the principal work of cannon had been the reduction of fortresses. Guns of all sizes were used in battering down walls. Field artillery consisted of such guns of the siege train as

[1] *Istoria d' Italia*, bk. I.
[2] *Arte della guerra*, bk. II (on arquebuses), bk. III (on field artillery).
[3] *Quesiti et inventioni*, bk. I, quesiti 8 and 11.

could be brought into the field[1], and, since this proportion varied according to the methods of transport
of the different armies, the nature of field artillery
could not be precisely defined. The Italian wars
modified the situation by diffusing among the armies
of Europe improved means of transport and by
forcing the gunners of the principal belligerents,
under the stress of competition, to approximate to
a common standard of mobility. In consequence
there grew up a rough distinction between siege
artillery and field artillery.

The bad roads of the period often made the problem
of transport a vital one. In the winter of 1521–2, for
instance, the French failed to reduce the city of Parma
simply because the condition of the roads prevented
them from bringing up their heavy guns[2]. The inadequacy of mountain roads for the transport of
artillery is shown by the incredible difficulties of
Charles VIII's passage of the Apennines in 1495[3],
and of Francis I's passage of the Alps in 1515[4]: in
each case an alert foe could have turned these difficulties to the destruction of the French. Nevertheless at this time the French army excelled all others
in mobility. Prior to the Italian wars several devices
had been adopted by the French monarchy to improve
the transport of its artillery. The most important

---

[1] Jähns, *Handbuch*, pp. 786 *seq.*
[2] Guicciardini, *Istoria d' Italia*, bk. xiv; Guicciardini was
governor of the besieged city.
[3] Commines, *Mémoires*, bk. viii, ch. v; Delavigne, *Voyage
de Naples*, p. 156.
[4] Giovio, *Istorie*, bk. xv.

of these was the adoption of the gun carriage,
or, in other words, the mounting of guns of every
size on permanent wheeled supports[1]. The result was
a greatly increased facility not only in transporting
but in laying the gun[2]. Another capital improvement
was the employment of horses—numerous, strong,
carefully chosen, and highly trained[3]. While the guns
of the Italians and the Spaniards were trundled
slowly over the country-side by lurching oxen[4], and
the emperor Maximilian had only sufficient draught-
animals to move half his siege-train at a time[5], the
sturdy French horses drew the heaviest cannon over
the most difficult ground, and equalled on a level
road the marching speed of fast cavalry[6]. The importance which the French attached to a mobile
artillery is also proved by their special efforts to
overcome unforeseen transport difficulties. On his
march to Naples Charles VIII assisted the convey-
ance of his siege train by hiring men and mules

[1] Giovio, *Istorie*, bk. xv; *Relazioni of the Venetian Ambassadors*, Series I, vol. iv, pp. i *seq.*, and cf. Series I, vol. vi, p. 16.

[2] Cf. Passero, *Giornali*, p. 68.

[3] Giovio, *Istorie*, bks. ii and xv. Portoveneri (*Memoriale*,
20 June 1496) mentions French ammunition wagons passing
through Pisa drawn by as many as 16 and 20 horses.

[4] Guicciardini, *Istoria d' Italia*, bk. xvii.

[5] Loyal Serviteur, *Histoire de Bayart*, ch. xxxii. Maximilian's failure to take Padua in 1509 was in great measure
due to the difficulty of moving his heavy guns. The delay in
their arrival gave the Venetians ample time to fortify the city;
when at last the guns arrived the season was well advanced,
and it was the fear that the autumn rains would prevent his
getting his guns away that caused him to break off the siege
so abruptly (see Bembo, *Istoria Viniziana*, bk. ix).

[6] Giovio, *Istorie*, bk. ii.

locally[1]. During the winter campaign of 1510 the French master of artillery succeeded in moving his guns over the snow by means of sledges of his own design[2]. In the course of his arduous journey over the Apennines in 1495 King Charles was advised to carry his guns in separate pieces[3]; though he did not entertain the proposal it is interesting to note that the imperialists did actually take their guns to pieces in their hurried return from Marseilles in 1524, and that even so they were obliged to leave one heavy gun buried on the line of march[4]. The big guns regulated the pace of all armies[5]. We find the viceroy of Naples in 1511[6], and St Pol in 1528[7], preparing for a long march by sending the siege artillery in advance.

The improvements in artillery transport introduced by the French were adopted in varying degrees by the other armies which fought in Italy[8]. The general result was not only the greater efficiency of the artillery arm, but also the ability to manoeuvre guns below a certain size on the field of battle, and

---

[1] Cf. Charles VIII's letter of 21 Dec. 1494.

[2] Floranges, *Mémoires*, bk. I, p. 60.

[3] Commines, *Mémoires*, bk. VIII, ch. V.

[4] Guicciardini, *Istoria d' Italia*, bk. XV.

[5] Cf. Charles VIII's letter of 4 Sept. 1495; Commines, *Mémoires*, bk. VIII, ch. VI.

[6] Passero, *Giornali*, p. 177.

[7] Guicciardini, *Istoria d' Italia*, bk. XIX.

[8] Cf. *Relazioni of the Venetian Ambassadors*, Series I, vol. VI, pp. 16 *seq.*; also the remark of Portoveneri, the Pisan diarist (*Memoriale*, 14 May 1496): "ad dì ditto, si mandò alcune bonbarde, chiamati passovolanti, a Ripafatta, li quali si portavano sulle carette, e così si trovano fatti in Pissa al usanza di Franza."

the consequent origin of the modern distinction between siege artillery and field artillery[1]. According
to Paolo Giovio the first commander to use artillery
in the field was Bartolommeo Colleoni, who died in
1475. He placed his guns behind his other arms and
fired them through gaps which were formed at the
sound of a trumpet[2]. Although guns were certainly
employed in battle at a period earlier than this,
nevertheless most Italians were impressed by Charles
VIII's use of field guns as by a novelty in warfare[3].
Other armies were not slow to imitate the French.
It was the custom in the early campaigns of the
Italian wars to post the guns in front of an army
drawn up for battle, and to restrict their firing to a
short preliminary bombardment, or merely to an
opening volley. When once battle was joined they
were usually masked by their own troops. This tradition moulded the artillery tactics of both sides at
Fornovo, at Cerignola, and at Agnadello. At Ravenna,
as we shall see later, there was a new development.

A further reason, besides lack of mobility, for
limiting the heavy cannon to siege work only, was
their comparative ineffectiveness against small targets.
With the rough methods of sighting then in vogue
it was very difficult for a big gun to hit a battalion
of infantry on the march[4], while no gun was able to

---

[1] Canestrini notes that the Florentine administration dis-
tinguishes between heavy and light guns by the year 1502
(*Scritti inediti di Machiavelli*, p. xxx).

[2] Giovio, *Elogi*, p. 139.

[3] Guicciardini, *Istoria d' Italia*, bk. I.

[4] Cf. Machiavelli, *Discorsi*, bk. II, ch. XVII.

fire with accuracy against objects on a different level from itself[1]. Infantry could usually shelter themselves from bombardment, as at Ravenna and Novara, by lying flat[2]. Several instances occur of successes won with remarkably small loss in the teeth of direct artillery fire[3]. It was therefore natural that a distinction should grow up between heavy guns reserved for siege work, such as the bombarda, the mortar, and the larger culverin, and guns of lesser calibre, such as the falcon, the smaller culverin and the spingarda, which were adapted also for work in the field[4].

The dividing line between field artillery and hand firearms was not made till the invention of the musket. During the first two decades of the Italian wars the transport of large arquebuses by horses and mules often caused them to be reckoned as a part of the artillery. Strictly speaking, however, this type of arquebus belonged to the category of small arms, since in battle it became the weapon of the infantry and was fitted with a hook in order that one man should be able to manipulate it unaided. It nevertheless remained so cumbersome in the field that at Ravenna the Spanish infantry attempted to use it in the manner of light artillery[5]. Pedro Navarro drew up in front of his men thirty wagons fitted with

[1] *E.g.* Lautrec's artillery at Troia in 1528 was ineffective against the enemy on higher ground (Giovio, *Istorie*, bk. xxv).

[2] Guicciardini, *Istoria d' Italia*, bk. x; Floranges, *Mémoires*, bk. I, p. 126.

[3] Cf. Loyal Serviteur, *Histoire de Bayart*, chh. xxxiii and l.

[4] Cf. Machiavelli, *Arte della guerra*, bk. iii.

[5] Coccinius, *De bellis italicis*, p. 228; Porto, *Lettere Storiche*, no. 66.

large arquebuses[1]. It is clear from the statements of contemporary writers that these wagons, although posted behind a ditch, were intended in case of necessity to be manoeuvred against the enemy. The failure of the Spaniards at Ravenna, which was due chiefly to the successful manoeuvring of the duke of Ferrara's field artillery, caused military opinion to abandon the idea of armed wagons and to rely instead on the mobility in battle of light guns. The decision was justified by the success of the French artillery at Marignano. Spanish ingenuity, however, continued to busy itself with the problem of the heavy arquebus. A solution was reached with the invention of the musket. Though the musket was heavier than the average arquebus, and though it was in consequence carried by horses on the march, the use of the forked rest made the musketeer more accurate than the arquebusier and less dependent on the conformation of the ground. The arrival of a portable firearm more mobile than the smallest cannon and effective only in the hands of the infantry produced a clear distinction between light guns and small arms. Indeed musketry fire proved so potent and reliable in battle that the later years of the sixteenth century are marked by a general neglect of field artillery[2].

The gradual character of the differentiation between the various classes of firearms must not be allowed to obscure the fact that Charles VIII's invasion produced a revolution in gunnery. In no other

[1] For a fuller discussion of these wagons see p. 185.
[2] Jähns, *Handbuch*, Vorblick.

branch of the military art did the Italian wars produce so abrupt a change. Before 1494 the Italian
princes, with the exception of the duke of Ferrara,
took little interest in artillery. The fame which Duke
Hercole of Ferrara acquired for his activity as a
designer of guns and as an artillerist testifies to his
neighbours' neglect of the subject[1]. Alfonso, who
succeeded Hercole in 1505, carried on the tradition
of his father and lived to save the reputation of
Italian gunnery. But not even the Ferrarese had
seen such guns as those which comprised the siege
train of Charles VIII—a siege train which earlier in
the century had been hammered into excellence by
a long war of liberation. In 1494 the Italians saw
gun-carriages for the first time. They saw guns that
could be sighted better than their own[2]. They saw
gunners who had been trained in special schools, who
were assisted by a numerous personnel[3], and whom
their fellow-soldiers held in honour[4]. Instead of the
iron guns firing stone or leaden balls to which they
were accustomed they saw huge bronze "cannoni"
firing iron balls the size of a man's head[5]. Above all
they were impressed by the quantity of the French

[1] Cf. Loyal Serviteur, *Histoire de Bayart*, ch. XLII; Floranges, *Mémoires*, bk. I, p. 72; also *Diario Ferrarese*, Feb. 1495.

[2] Giovio, *Istorie*, bk. II.

[3] Delavigne, *Voyage de Naples*, p. 156, mentions among the
personnel of the French artillery "Canonniers, Chargeurs,
Cartiers, Aydes, Boutefeux, Arbalestriers, gens à pied suivans
ladite artillerie, Pionniers, Maçons, Mareschaux, Serruriers, et
autres gens de toutes pratiques destinez et propres au faict
deladite artillerie."

[4] Giovio, *Istorie*, bk. XV.

[5] Giovio, *Istorie*, bk. II; Guicciardini, *Istoria d' Italia*, bk. I.

artillery: King Charles brought with him more guns
than had ever been seen together in Italy before.
All historians bear witness to the ascendancy of the
French artillery over that of the Italians. Hitherto,
owing to the small size of the Italian guns, to their
comparative rarity, and, above all, to their slow rate
of fire, fortresses had often been able to defy the
utmost efforts of the besieger. Now, the fury of the
French guns and heavy mortars quickly reduced the
most formidable strongholds. Citadels which had
previously held out for months fell in a few hours[1].
Many garrisons surrendered at the mere threat of
bombardment. The contrast between Charles's easy
triumph over the kingdom of Naples and its pro-
tracted and toilsome recovery by Ferdinand gives us
a measure of the superiority of the French artillery
over that of contemporary armies[2].

The French artillery maintained its ascendancy
throughout the earlier Italian campaigns. At Fornovo
its mere reputation weakened the resolution of the
Italian attack, and though French writers protest
that their guns on that day were poorly handled, the
Italians confess to having suffered more casualties
from the hostile artillery than their own gunners inflicted on the enemy[3]. It was French gunnery which
prevented Florence from recovering Pisa in 1495[4].

[1] All this is especially emphasized by Guicciardini, bks. I
and xv.

[2] This contrast is brought out by Priuli, De bello gallico.

[3] Cf. Commines, Mémoires, bk. viii, ch. vi; Benedetti, Il
fatto d' arme del Tarro, bk. i; Priuli, De bello gallico; Cagnola,
Storia di Milano.

[4] Guicciardini, Storia Fiorentina, pp. 137–8.

Ludovico Sforza tried to withstand Louis XII in 1500 by borrowing guns from the duke of Ferrara[1]: his failure was recognized by contemporaries as a further tribute to the power of the French artillery[2]. At Agnadello the superiority of the French guns was marked[3]: at Ravenna (1512) and Marignano (1515) it was decisive.

From the first the successes of the French artillery caused a general improvement in the artillery of the Italian states. As soon as King Ferdinand had ejected the invader from his realm, he set about increasing his supply of artillery and improving its design[4]. The Florentines manned their guns in the Pisan war with skilled gunners from Piedmont, Germany, and France[5]. The duke of Ferrara continued to cast cannon with great industry. In 1510 he was privileged to render vital assistance to the best artillerymen in the world, for in that year the French reduced Legnago mainly by means of two Ferrarese guns of immense size, one of which the duke had cast with his own hands[6]. In the preceding year he had gained the most famous artillery success of the age. Against the Venetian fleet which sailed up the Po to within a few miles of his capital he brought out guns by land and water. He posted them so skilfully and protected them so efficiently that when they opened fire the

---

[1] Priuli, *De bello gallico*.
[2] Cf. Pitti, *Istoria Fiorentina*, bk. I, p. 66.
[3] Porto, *Lettere Storiche*, no. 16; Floranges, *Mémoires*, bk. I, p. 31.
[4] Giovio, *Istorie*, bk. III.
[5] Canestrini, *Scritti inediti di Machiavelli*, p. xxx.
[6] Giovio, *Vita Alfonsi Ferrariae*.

ships were unable either to retaliate or to escape[1]. The moral effect of the victory was very great, for the fleet was the symbol of the far-flung Venetian power, and that fleet had been annihilated by a princeling who knew how to use guns.

The development of gunnery was accompanied by an increase in matériel. Although the contemporary habit of counting arquebuses as small artillery makes it difficult to discover the exact number of guns in any given action, nevertheless the occasional record of the quantity of heavy artillery, as distinct from light cannon and small arms, gives a fair indication of the rate of increase. The increase seems to have occurred for the most part before the peace of Noyon (1516): little change is noticeable in the campaigns of 1521–8. For instance, the number of heavy guns in the four French expeditions of 1494, 1507, 1515, and 1524 varied thus: thirty-six[2], sixty[3], seventy-two[4], seventy[5]. On the last occasion guns were taken from the fortresses of sorely-tried France in order to swell the total. At three important and typical sieges

[1] Guicciardini, *Istoria d' Italia*, bk. VIII; Bembo, *Istoria Viniziana*, bk. IX; Mocenico, *La guerra di Cambrai*, bk. II. The duke sheltered his guns behind the embankment of the river; the high level of the water, due to the autumn rains, made the ships an easy target.

[2] Giovio, *Istorie*, bk. II. There were again 36 guns with the French expedition against Naples in 1501 (D'Auton, *Chroniques de Louis XII*, 1501, ch. II). Sanuto says that there were 40 guns on carriages on the earlier occasion (*La spedizione di Carlo VIII*, bk. I).

[3] Floranges, *Mémoires*, bk. I.

[4] *Ibid.*

[5] Sanuto, *Diarii*, 24 Oct. 1524, vol. XXXVII, col. 102.

the number of siege guns is given as follows: seventeen at Novara in 1495[1], thirty-six at Verona in 1515[2], about forty at Pavia in 1528[3]. An eyewitness of Maximilian's siege of Padua in 1509 estimates the number of his heavy guns as between six and seven score[4]. Whether this very high figure be accepted or not, it may be taken as confirming the many historians who insist on the exceptional character of that famous siege. Although contemporaries dwell on the enormous size of guns used on certain occasions—as, for instance, at this same siege of Padua[5]— there does not appear to have been any marked or progressive growth in calibre between 1494 and 1528. Except for an evident decline in the popularity of the heavy siege mortar the general character of the artillery during this period remained unchanged. Historians occasionally draw attention to an exceptionally large cannon as a marvel, but never as a novelty. Thus we are told of a culverin with a remarkably long range which defended Genoa in 1514[6], but elsewhere we read that a very similar weapon was in use at Vico Pisano in 1495[7]. In the same way Filippino Doria's terrible basilisk, which

[1] Benedetti, *Il fatto d' arme del Tarro*, bk. II.

[2] Guicciardini, *Istoria d' Italia*, bk. XII.

[3] *Ibid.* bk. XIX. The Venetian heavy guns, probably less than half the total, numbered 20.

[4] Loyal Serviteur, *Histoire de Bayart*, ch. XXXVIII. Buonaccorsi, *Diario*, p. 143, and Nardi, *Istorie della città di Firenze*, bk. IV, confirm this statement to the extent of saying that Maximilian's guns of all sizes numbered about 200.

[5] Loyal Serviteur, ch. XXXII.

[6] Senarega, *De rebus genuensibus commentaria* 1513–14.

[7] Giovio, *Istorie*, bk. III.

laid low forty men with one shot in 1528[1], is more
than matched by the basilisks with which the Great
Captain ruined the massive walls of Cephalonia nearly
thirty years before[2]. It is not without interest to
note a new use for heavy artillery which was suggested by the long range of some of the larger guns.
At Bologna in 1512 and in Venetia in 1514 Raymundo
de Cardona, the viceroy of Naples, bombarded at
long range a civilian population which he could not
reach by more direct methods. His reasons, as given
by contemporaries who unite in condemning his
action, have a curiously modern ring. On the earlier
occasion he hoped by terrorizing the population into
surrender to escape the inconveniences of a formal
siege[3]. On the later occasion his sole object was to
perpetuate the memory of his invasion[4].

It remains to consider the progress which was
made in artillery tactics. With regard to the use of
artillery in siegecraft and fortification the expedition
of Charles VIII produced an unstable situation which
was restored to equilibrium only after many years
of warfare. The immediate result of the conquest of
Naples was a general disbelief in the power of fortresses to withstand the new heavy siege guns. The
twin citadels of Naples were so overawed by the
preliminary havoc wrought by the French siege
train that they surrendered without waiting for the

---

[1] According to Guicciardini, *Istoria d' Italia*, bk. XIX.
[2] In 1500: Giovio, *Vita Consalvi Cordubae*, bk. I.
[3] Porto, *Lettere Storiche*, no. 61.
[4] "acciochè fosse più chiara la memoria di questa espedi-
zione" (Guicciardini, *Istoria d' Italia*, bk. XI).

final assault[1]. In 1503 the garrison of Ceri insisted on capitulating to Cesare Borgia on the ground that to hold out longer against so furious a bombardment meant certain annihilation[2]. Soldiers soon realized, however, that the guns which reduced a stronghold so easily could also be used in its defence, and with the recognition of this truth siege warfare became gradually stabilized into a prolonged conflict between well-matched artilleries. It is notable in this connexion that the designer of the new citadel of Genoa, built after the revolt of that city from France in 1507, was Louis XII's grand master of artillery[3].

The object of the gunners who defended a besieged town was twofold: to harass the enemy during the preliminary bombardment and to check him at the final assault. The harassing fire to which besieging artillery was subjected often forced besiegers even before 1494 to shelter their guns in trenches. With the progress of the Italian wars the construction of strong defences for siege guns became more and more necessary and the duration of sieges more and more prolonged. As early as 1495 first the French and then the Neapolitan artillery was forced by accurate fire from the Castel Nuovo at Naples to dig trenches for its own protection[4]. The artillery which bombarded Novara in the same year was screened with

[1] Delavigne, *Voyage de Naples*, p. 132.
[2] Giustinian, *Dispaccio* 341.
[3] Loyal Serviteur, *Histoire de Bayart*, ch. XXVII.
[4] Delavigne, *Voyage de Naples*, p. 135; Giovio, *Istorie*, bk. III.

clods and fascines[1]—an old and simple device. The
Spanish guns which besieged Taranto in 1501 were
posted behind high ramparts[2]. The Florentine artillery engaged in the reduction of Pisa made use of
gabions[3]. The violence of the gunfire from Padua in
1509 forced Maximilian to dig trenches for both his
artillery and his infantry[4]. At another siege of the
same city in 1513 the besiegers were constrained to
entrench their artillery at a great distance from the
walls and to push it gradually forward under cover
of fresh digging operations[5]. From this time on the
bombardment of a city is a slow and laborious process, and only those guns which are adequately protected or hidden can approach the walls closely enough
to make a breach. The failure of the siege of Marseilles in 1524 was due among other causes to the
stony nature of the ground which prevented the
adequate entrenching of the artillery[6].

The garrisons of Italian towns soon discovered the
value of flanking artillery for the defence of a breach
in the walls. For guns so posted it became customary
to build specially sited platforms (*piatte forme*) and
specially strengthened parapets (*cavalieri*). In 1501
the Faventini, besieged by Cesare Borgia, broke
many violent assaults by means of well-placed artillery

---

[1] Benedetti, *Il fatto d' arme del Tarro*, bk. II.

[2] Giovio, *Vita Consalvi Cordubae*, bk. I.

[3] Pitti, *Vita di Antonio Giacomini*, p. 233 (in the *Arch. Stor.
It.*, vol. IV, pt. II).

[4] Porto, *Lettere Storiche*, no. 27; Bembo, *Istoria Viniziana*,
bk. IX; Mocenico, *La guerra di Cambrai*, bk. II.

[5] Giovio, *Istorie*, bk. XII.

[6] Giovio, *Vita Marchionis Piscariae*, bk. IV.

enfilading the breach[1]. Similar methods repulsed Foix from Ravenna in 1512[2], Trivulzio from Brescia in 1515[3], and Lautrec from Verona in 1516[4]. The guns most suited to such work seem to have been large culverins. With the spread of hand firearms and their increased co-operation in the defence of towns, the labour of making a breach paled before the difficulty of carrying it.

In the course of the Italian wars the methods of gunners engaged in siege work passed through two phases. Their first reply to the increased efficiency of the defence was to accentuate the violence of the bombardment. An eyewitness of the furious bombardment of the Castel Nuovo in 1495 states that the French fired over 300 shots in the space of three hours[5]. In 1500 a detachment of French troops sent to help Florence against Pisa was accompanied by twenty-two[6] heavy guns with which they threw down 120 feet of wall in the space of one day[7]. At Verona in 1516 the combined artilleries of France and Venice, consisting of 120 guns[8], fired 20,000 iron cannon-balls in eleven days and ruined a stretch of wall 300 paces long[9]. Nevertheless the besiegers, though their

---

[1] Guicciardini, *Istoria d' Italia*, bk. v.
[2] Giovio, *Vita Alfonsi Ferrariae*.
[3] Giovio, *Istorie*, bk. XVI. [4] *Ibid*. bk. XVIII.
[5] Delavigne, *Voyage de Naples*, p. 137.
[6] Pitti, *Istoria Fiorentina*, bk. I, p. 68 (in the *Arch. Stor. It.*). Buonaccorsi says 22 falconetti and 4 cannoni (*Diario*, p. 31).
[7] Guicciardini, *Istoria d' Italia*, bk. v; Pitti (*loc. cit.*) and Buonaccorsi (*loc. cit.*) say 80 feet.
[8] Floranges, *Mémoires*, bk. I, p. 290.
[9] Giovio, *Istorie*, bk. XVIII.

operations were directed by Lautrec, "the stormer of cities[1]," were unable to take the town.

In subsequent campaigns there was a tendency to substitute for this sheer weight of metal a more careful posting of the guns. Much of course depended on the besieged town's geographical situation. Often it was impossible for the besiegers to find positions from which their artillery could dominate the defence. It became customary, however, to study the topography of the neighbourhood more carefully than in former days, and cities otherwise impregnable sometimes succumbed to the skilful use by gunners of favouring ground. It was in the French expedition against Genoa in 1507 that the value of this new method was first clearly shown. The Genoese took up a strong position which blocked the mountainous approach to their city. The French, unable to dislodge them by a frontal attack, managed with great labour to haul two heavy guns on to the high ground on the flanks and to compel them by well-directed fire to withdraw[2]. At the siege of Verona in 1510 the Venetian artillery was so advantageously placed on commanding ground in the neighbourhood of the city, that the guns of the defence were silenced[3]; vigorous sorties, however, were sufficient to discourage the cautious soldiers of St Mark from advancing

---

[1] See Giovio, *Elogi*, bk. VI.

[2] Guicciardini, *Istoria d' Italia*, bk. VII. D'Auton, *Chroniques de Louis XII*, 1506–7, ch. XXII, says that 4 falcons were hauled up on to the flanks, while 2 gros cannons fired from the foot of the mountain.

[3] Guicciardini, *Istoria d' Italia*, bk. IX.

to the assault. The marquis of Pescara adopted these tactics whenever the conditions of the siege allowed. They suited the genius of a commander who always preferred skill and neatness to brute force—whose method resembled a rapier rather than a bludgeon. In 1517 he reduced the citadel of Sora, which was reputed impregnable, by hauling guns into what had been regarded as impossible places[1]. At the siege of Como in 1521 he supplemented the fire of his artillery with arquebus and musketry fire from the roofs of buildings[2]. When he captured Genoa in the following year he brought the new tactics to perfection. Heavy guns, posted with much labour on high ground overlooking the walls, opened fire as the storming troops advanced, silenced the guns of the defence, and broke up hostile formations which were drawn up in readiness to counterattack[3]. The contrast between this scientific bombardment and the sullen poundings of a generation before affords a good illustration of the way in which the restless spirit of the Renaissance upset military routine.

A similar change from convention to adaptability characterized the employment of artillery in the field. The fifteenth century practice of placing the artillery in front of the other arms and of restricting its work to a preliminary cannonade gave place to manoeuvring and participation in all the phases of the battle. At Fornovo both armies adhered to the old method. At

---

[1] Giovio, *Vita Marchionis Piscariae*, bk. I.
[2] *Ibid.* bk. II.
[3] *Ibid.* bk. III.

Cerignola there was a slight modification. Each army placed its artillery in front and opened the action with a cannonade, but, since Nemours adopted an echelon formation, and since his artillery was in front of his centre, his gunners were able to give covering fire to his forward wing[1]. Covering fire again appeared at the Garigliano, where the French built their bridge and secured their bridgehead under the protection of their guns[2]. At Agnadello, where the opposing artilleries faced each other across a river-bed, the French gunners outclassed the Venetians but did not contribute decisively to the final victory. The battle of Ravenna marks an epoch in the history of field artillery. It opened in the traditional manner with a mutual bombardment of fronting artilleries, but this bombardment, instead of ceasing when battle was fairly joined, continued to develop till it dominated the whole action. The preliminary cannonade lasted for the unusually long period of three hours and caused unprecedented casualties to both sides. This fact alone seems to show that the commanders on that day were expecting exceptional work from their gunners. The French commander at any rate was not disappointed. At the end of the second hour the duke of Ferrara worked some of the French guns round to a position on the flank and to the rear of the enemy. The peculiar deadliness of flanking fire at last forced the Spanish cavalry to abandon their entrenchments and to take the field in a very shaken

[1] Giovio, *Vita Consalvi Cordubae*, bk. II.
[2] Machiavelli, *Legazione XIII*, doc. 26.

condition. There they met with a swift defeat which involved the remainder of the army in ruin[1].

The effect of the battle of Ravenna on military opinion is reflected in the three succeeding battles of Novara, Marignano, and Bicocca, each of which consisted in the main of an attempt by the Swiss to capture the guns of their opponents. At Novara they were successful because they were able to screen their approach and to distract the fire of the enemy by a ruse; but their victory was gained only at the cost of severe losses from the French guns[2]. At Marignano their losses were even more severe and their object unattained. On the first day of this battle Francis I repulsed the Swiss by manoeuvring some of his artillery on to their flanks; on the second day the fire of his artillery was mainly frontal, as was that of the few Swiss guns, but its devastating effect at close range and its careful co-operation with the action of other arms were the chief causes of the French victory[3]. Neither at Bicocca nor at Pavia did artillery play a decisive part. At Bicocca the impatience of the Swiss, and at Pavia the impatience of King Francis, prevented an effective use of the French guns[4]. The imperialists, on the other hand, owed their victory on both occasions chiefly to their bold use of the improved infantry firearms. The French,

[1] For a fuller discussion of this battle see Appendix A.

[2] Floranges, *Mémoires*, bk. i; Guicciardini, *Istoria d' Italia*, bk. xi; Giovio, *Istorie*, bk. xii.

[3] Du Bellay, *Mémoires*, bk. i; Floranges, *Mémoires*, bk. i; Barrillon, *Journal*, ch. i.

[4] Guicciardini, *Istoria d' Italia*, bks. xiv and xv.

who had first shown to the world the capabilities of field artillery, proved themselves in the long run poorer tacticians than the Spaniards, whose vital weapon was the musket. This circumstance explains that neglect of field artillery which marked the later decades of the sixteenth century.

CHAPTER VI

TACTICS

TACTICS is the art of handling troops in immediate contact with the enemy. In battle a commander has to ask himself two questions: How am I to dispose the different parts of my army? and, In what sequence shall I bring those different parts into the fight? These two considerations, the one involving problems of space and the other problems of time, are fundamental to all military engagements. When an army is composed of simple elements, the solution of these problems is correspondingly easy. When, as in modern times, an army consists of many highly specialized classes of men and machinery, the great number of possible tactical combinations tends to eliminate from battles that quality of routine which was characteristic of the less complex fighting of earlier times. It is a phase in this change from simple to more complex tactics which we have to consider in the present chapter.

Under the Roman Empire, as in the Middle Ages, armies consisted of a mass of heavy shock troops trained for hand-to-hand fighting and an auxiliary force of more mobile troops armed for the most part with missile weapons. In each case the simplicity of the elements involved led to the rise of a customary tactical method. The Romans placed their unmounted shock troops in the centre and their light cavalry on the wings. In the Middle Ages, when the shock troops were mounted, the rôle of the light auxiliaries—the infantry—was usually almost negligible in battle: it comprised either vague skirmishing on the flanks of the cavalry or merely the guarding of the baggage in rear. Even with such simple elements as these, much depended on the timing of the action of each part of the army. It was the custom of the Romans, who fully realized the danger of risking the fortune of the day in one combined and simultaneous effort, to withhold a portion of the army from the fight and to give it the special duties of coming to the aid of the remainder if necessary and of adding force to the decisive blow when the enemy showed signs of weakening. Vegetius, the authoritative military writer of the later Roman Empire, says of the practice of maintaining adequate reserves in rear: "hac dispositione nulla melior invenitur[1]." Such prudence was not characteristic of mediaeval warfare. The soldiers of that age preferred to "put it to the touch, to gain or lose it all." Nevertheless the custom which grew up of organizing armies in two or three sections, called "battles," seems to show that commanders realized vaguely the advantage of being able to husband a part of their forces.

The Italian wars, which bridge the gulf between mediaeval and modern warfare, were characterized by an increasing complexity in military method. We have seen how the new weapons introduced by the invention of gunpowder were at this time classified

[1] Vegetius, *De re militari*, bk. III, ch. XVII.

and improved, and how both infantry and cavalry bifurcated into light-armed and heavy-armed troops. A result of this increased complexity was an increase in the number and difficulty of tactical problems. The same two questions continued to arise—the questions of place and of time in the correlation of the different activities of the army—but these activities were now so multifarious that an answer was reached only after painful experiment, and even then men were indisposed to accept it as final.

The divisions called "battles" of a mediaeval army were usually three in number—the vanguard, the main body (usually described as "the battle" par excellence), and the rearguard. Although these divisions were apparently less tactical than administrative, Machiavelli exaggerates when, writing in 1513, he describes the "battle" as a purely administrative unit[1]. At that time the "battle" still had a distinct tactical significance. In action it had been usual for each "battle" to seek out and fight the corresponding "battle" of the enemy, but by the end of the fifteenth century commanders were beginning to make better use of the elasticity which followed subdivision. Philippe de Clèves, writing in 1498, recommends the formation of three "battles" consisting of all arms, and adds that if the enemy has a lesser number than this, it is advisable to hold back one "battle" as a reserve[2]. Della Valle, writing in 1521, has a still

---

[1] *Discorsi*, bk. II, ch. XVI.
[2] *Instruction de toutes les manieres de guerroyer*, pt. II, pp. 82 seq. (Paris, 1558).

surer grasp of the advantage of subdivision. Whatever be the size of the army, he says, the only satisfactory organization for battle is to divide it into a number of units (*battaglioni*) and to put vigour into the attack[1]. Note should be taken of the change of attitude produced by twenty years of fighting. Whereas the organization of an army in administrative units suggests to Philippe de Clèves their employment for tactical purposes, della Valle is led to demand such an organization by tactical considerations alone.

It was the Swiss who first showed that subdivision had a tactical value. They adopted the customary division into three "battles," but from the first they regarded the "battle" as primarily a tactical unit. Each was organized similarly as a solid square, and victory was sought by a co-ordination of their action in the attack. Sometimes as at Cerignola[2] the three squares would advance in echelon, in which case the centre and the rear divisions carried out quite unmistakably the respective functions of support and reserve. At other times, as at Novara[3] and Marignano[4], frontal attacks were combined with diversions on the enemy's flank or rear. Although the Swiss introduced this important tactical principle of divided but co-ordinated action they failed to exploit it to the full. They owed their early victories to their exceptional mobility and elasticity, and when other nations by

---

[1] *Libro continente appertenentie ad capitanii*, bk. III, chh. XXXI–XXXIII.

[2] Giovio, *Vita Consalvi Cordubae*, bk. II.

[3] *Ibid.* bk. XII.   [4] *Ibid.* bk. XV.

imitating them produced infantries which threatened
to be their equals in the field, they did not try to
retain the advantage by improving on their traditional system. In the early years of the Italian wars
it was recognized that, provided they had space in
which to deploy, they were "a wall against the enemy
and almost unconquerable[1]"; but where the terrain
interfered with their formation they had been known
to give ground even before the despised levies of the
king of Naples[2]. This conservatism was no doubt
partly due to their confining themselves to infantry
action only. As befitted a race of mountaineers their
army was always essentially an infantry army. Sometimes in later years they were accompanied by
cavalry and a few guns, but no skill was ever shown
in supporting the infantry with these arms[3].

Lack of enterprise thus robbed the Swiss of the
opportunity of studying a second method of tactical
combination of no less moment than the co-operation
of separate units. This method was the co-operation
of separate arms. The old "battles" which the Swiss
taught commanders to handle in carefully correlated
attacks, consisted usually of all arms, but the habit
of envisaging an engagement in parts led naturally
to an analysis of the duties of the different arms, to
an assessment of their respective contributions to
victory, and so to their employment independently
of the "battles" to which they belonged. It was thus

[1] Guicciardini, *Istoria d' Italia*, bk. 1.
[2] At Rapallo, 1494; see Guicciardini, *Istoria d' Italia*, bk. 1.
[3] These remarks apply to the Swiss when acting as an independent force.

on two quite distinct principles that the component parts of armies came to be re-classified and re-combined for tactical purposes. Commanders studied not only where and when to use the different units into which their force was divided, but also where and when to use the different arms which it contained. The distinction is well brought out by the action of the Swiss at Bicocca. Though they were themselves the pioneers of the doctrine of combination between units in battle, they nevertheless so far failed to grasp the importance of co-operation between arms that they refused to postpone their attack till the French artillery could support them against what proved to be overwhelming odds.

At the opening of the Italian wars the position of the different arms in the battle array and their rôle during the fight were still matters of routine. It was usual for each "battle" to be organized with the massed infantry in the centre, the cavalry on the wings, and the artillery in front[1]. Light infantry and light cavalry would remain in open order on the flanks and immediately behind the guns. This formation assumed that the artillery and the missile weapons of the light troops would open a fight which was to be developed and decided by the shock tactics of the heavy cavalry and pikemen. Armies continued to be drawn up for battle on similar principles throughout the period of the Italian wars. Sometimes the

[1] The artillery was often attached to one "battle" only, as in the French army at Cerignola, or to two of the three "battles," as in the French army at Fornovo.

"battles" were arranged in depth, as at Ravenna[1]
in 1512, and sometimes in line, as at Troia[2] in 1527,
but in spite of such minor variations there is discernible at the opening of all important engagements
the orthodox battle-order inherited from the preceding age. Within this shell of routine, however,
there occurred between 1494 and 1528 many new developments in the art of handling troops in contact
with the enemy. The developments which were
internal to each particular arm we have already
considered. It remains now to examine the more
important battles of the Italian wars with a view to
discovering what improvements were made in the
art of combining the action of these arms as inter-
dependent members of a single military organism.
We are inquiring, in other words, how far commanders
in the Italian wars learned to make the most of the
forces at their disposal.

Before descending to particulars it will be well to
notice the appearance of three new features in the
tactics of the period. Each marks a break with
mediaeval tradition. In the first place there is a
notable increase in military prudence. One manifestation of this is the growth of the habit of forming a
reserve. At the battle of Fornovo the Italians employed an elaborate system of local and general
reserves, and attributed their failure to the death
early in the fight of the commander whose duty it

[1] In the case of the army of the Holy League (see Guicciardini, *Istoria d' Italia*, bk. x).
[2] In the case of the French army (see Du Bellay, *Mémoires*,
bk. III, p. 66).

was to bring these into action[1]. At Ravenna the reserve left in rear by the French was able, at a later
stage in the fight, to render service which was important and perhaps decisive[2]. Another manifestation
of the growth of military prudence is the rise of the
custom of fortifying the field of battle. The ditch dug
by the Spaniards at Cerignola was said by Fabrizio
Colonna to have gained them the victory[3], and in
subsequent campaigns the practice was extended till
at last every battle took the form of an attack on an
entrenched camp.

A second feature of the tactics of the Italian wars
was an increase in the adaptability of armies in
action. This change is of course very closely con-
nected with the increase in elasticity which has already
been noticed. Mediaeval battles contained an element
of ritual. There were certain recognized ways of employing troops and certain courses of action which it
was customary to follow. Survivals of this attitude
are seen in the practice of confining the rôle of field
guns to a preliminary cannonade and in the contempt
of the Swiss for artificial protective works. The break
with tradition which appears in the thought of the
Renaissance appears also in the wars of the Renaissance. The younger commanders employ methods

---

[1] The commander in question was Ridolfo Gonzaga (Guicciardini, *Istoria d' Italia*, bk. II).   [2] *Ibid.* bk. X.
[3] Giovio, *Vita Consalvi Cordubae*, bk. II: "Io ho udito dire
al Signor Fabritio Colonna, quando egli contava il successo di
quella battaglia, che la vittoria quel giorno non era stata in
altra importanza d' industria di soldati, nè di valore di Capitano generale; ma solo nello spatio d' un picciolo argine, e d' un
bassissima fossa" (Italian translation, Venice, 1561).

less because they are sanctioned by custom than because they are best suited to achieve the object in
view. Thus the marquis of Pescara by a bold experiment in the tactical employment of infantry wins
Italy for his sovereign. Even in the use of traditional
methods there appears a new flexibility—a power to
improvise for the occasion. At this time the French
army was in many ways more attached than its rivals
to the military doctrines of the past, yet it was
Francis I who gave at Marignano the supreme example at this period of that quick conformity to
changing circumstances, that mastery of a threatening
situation by swift decision on the field of battle, for
which the French command has since become justly
celebrated.

The third and most important change in the
character of European tactics resulted from that
shifting of the military outlook of which many other
effects have already appeared. Perhaps it may be
best described by saying that the desire to win tended
to exceed the desire to fight. Much of the fighting of
the Middle Ages had been undertaken more for the
love of fighting and from a spirit of adventure than
in order to achieve definite political results. Such a
spirit can be descried behind the English aggression
in France, and such a spirit animated in an even more
pronounced fashion the mercenary companies to
which that aggression gave birth. The spirit was
perpetuated when the early mercenary captains be-
queathed their detached professional standpoint to
the Italian condottieri, and when in 1494 all that

survived of knight-errantry in France joined the
great adventure of Charles VIII. But with the pro-
longation of the Italian wars, and the growth of the
quarrel between Hapsburg and Valois, there came
the modern view of war as a means to a political end.
Commanders look beyond victory to the fruits of
victory. They fight not for glory but for the possession
of Italy. Especially is this attitude reflected in the
later Italian battles. Any expedient is used which
will compass the defeat of the enemy. Attempts are
made to take the enemy by surprise, as when Pescara's men, clothed in white, crept into the park at
Pavia[1]. Ruses are employed, as when Lautrec's men-
at-arms donned the imperial red cross at Bicocca[2].
Such stratagems were not new—indeed they are as
old as the art of war itself—but they had been dis-
couraged by the spirit of the Middle Ages, which inclined to let God decide the issue in a fair fight, and
savoured rather of the rationalizing mood which was
at this time divorcing secular interests from ethical
teaching. Perhaps the most important aspect of the
new spirit was the desire to exploit victory to the
full. To mediaeval soldiers the pursuit of a beaten
enemy was scarcely honourable because unchivalrous.
To a modern commander a relentless hunting of a

[1] See the letter of 27 Feb. 1525 "mandata a Napoli per lo
scrivano di ratione dell' esercito della Cesarea Maestà" quoted
in Passero, *Giornali*, p. 321.
[2] Guicciardini, *Istoria d' Italia*, bk. xiv. Cf. also the action
of the Venetians in putting on the livrée taken from the French
dead when they attempted to rush Legnago in 1510 (see Buonaccorsi, *Diario*, pp. 151–2).

retreating enemy is the one excuse for overtaxing the strength of his own men[1]. The modern view was represented by Gonsalvo de Cordova in his untiring pursuit of the French from the Garigliano, by Pescara at the harrying of Bonnivet across the Sesia, and by the prince of Orange when, issuing from Naples in 1528, he fell upon and broke the wretched remnant of the army of Lautrec. The French, on the other hand, failed consistently to exploit their victories. At Fornovo Charles VIII refused to press a demoralized enemy[2]; at Ravenna by the death of Gaston de Foix the French army was hamstrung in mid-career; at Marignano Francis I deliberately chose to let the Swiss escape. A report has been preserved to us of the views for and against pursuit which were brought forward in the king's council after this last battle. Against the argument that the moment of victory offered the best opportunity for humbling an arrogant enemy, councillors who carried weight with the king urged that it was unchivalrous to slay a foe who was half-dead—nay, that it was preferable to aid him by building a golden bridge for his retreat[3]. These views show clearly the opposition between the old and the new military morality, and it is worthy of note that in the long run the side which the more completely freed itself from the atmosphere of past centuries was the side which gained the hegemony of Italy.

[1] Cf. *Infantry Training*, 1914, p. 147.

[2] Giovio, *Istorie*, bk. II.

[3] " J'ai ouï dire à tous bons capitaines et gens savants en guerre que à son ennemi on doit faire un pont d'or pour fuir" (Barrillon, *Journal*, ch. I, pp. 128–36).

In the ensuing consideration of the chief battles of the Italian wars attention will be focussed mainly on the co-ordination of those different arms of which the particular employment has been considered in detail in earlier chapters.

Fornovo (1495).

At the battle of Fornovo[1] the French were attacked while on the march along the bank of the river Taro. The river was on their right, and the Italian army was ahead of them on the other side of the river. The French army, which expected the attack, was organized as a vanguard, a main body, and a rearguard; these divisions marched one behind another, with spaces of about a quarter of a mile between them. Each "battle" was composed of both infantry and cavalry, but the vanguard was especially strengthened with Swiss and German pikemen in close formation. The artillery was placed along the right flank of the two leading "battles"; it was thus nearest to the river and to the quarter from which the enemy was expected. The Italians worked out a very complicated plan of attack which it is not easy to understand from the accounts of contemporary historians. The essence of their plan was to tell off three mixed forces

[1] See Commines, *Mémoires*, bk. VIII, ch. VI; Delavigne, *Voyage de Naples*, p. 158; Benedetti, *Il fatto d' arme del Tarro*, bk. I; Letter of Pointet (in La Pilorgerie, *Campagne et bulletins de Charles VIII*, p. 351); Guicciardini, *Istoria d' Italia*, bk. II; Giovio, *Istorie*, bk. II; Sanuto, *La spedizione di Carlo VIII*, bk. IV, and a letter therein quoted, p. 535; Priuli, *De bello gallico*; Bembo, *Istoria Viniziana*, bk. II; Malipiero, *Annali Veneti*; Oricellarius, *De bello italico*.

of infantry and cavalry to cross the river and attack simultaneously each of the three French "battles"; another force, consisting of stradiots only, was sent across the river behind the French rearguard with orders to make a circuit and to fall upon the French left flank. A reserve was assigned to each of the three forces intended for the direct attack, while a large force was left in rear as a general reserve and camp guard. The guns were placed along the bank facing directly across the river towards the French. The subsequent battle brought little credit to either side. The Italian gunnery was ineffectual. The three main attacking parties were held back till the French had almost passed, and, when launched, were badly broken up by the steep river banks before they gained contact with the enemy. Each was repulsed by the French, and each returned across the river without calling upon its reserve. The diversion by the stradiots on the French left developed into a looting of the French baggage. The French did not pursue, but contented themselves with bombarding the Italian camp as they continued their march. The actual hand-to-hand fighting lasted little more than fifteen minutes, while the whole action occupied about one hour.

This battle is notable for the bad choice of ground by the Italians and for the over-elaboration of their tactical scheme. Lack of determination prevented them from driving their attacks home or from making use of their reserves, while indiscipline ruined the most promising feature of the whole plan—the diversion of the stradiots. Other points worthy of comment are the promiscuous mixture of cavalry with infantry in the main offensive, and the very secondary rôle played by the artillery of both sides.

Cerignola (1503).

At Cerignola[1] Gonsalvo's army was drawn up on a straight front behind a ditch. It was divided into six parts with cavalry on the wings and in reserve. Spaces were left between the different sections through which the cavalry reserve could advance when called upon. The Spanish artillery was placed in front of the other arms along the edge of the ditch. The French advanced in three "battles" arranged in echelon, with their forward wing on the right. To the centre were assigned the duties of a true tactical support, namely, to assist the advance of the right first with artillery fire and then by joining battle on its left. The rear wing, which consisted of cavalry, was held in reserve. The obstacle of the ditch enabled the Spaniards to beat off the attack of the French right and centre. Night fell, and the French commander was killed before the reserve wing of the echelon could be brought into action. In the darkness and confusion the French army disintegrated and fled. Both the attack and the defence at Cerignola were an improvement on the tactics of Fornovo.

---

[1] Guicciardini, *Istoria d' Italia*, bk. v; Giovio, *Istorie*, bk. VIII; Grumello (whose brother was present), *Cronaca*, cap. XI; Giustinian, *Dispaccio* 375, reflects the earliest contemporary version of the fight.

Each side understood the necessity of an adequate reserve, and each distinguished between the rôles of cavalry and infantry in the battle. Moreover, while the Spanish artillery carried out the customary duty of a mere preliminary bombardment, the French made a new tactical departure by covering with their guns the advance of the infantry.

Agnadello (1509).

The scene of the battle of Agnadello[1] was very similar to that of the action at Fornovo. In the course of a series of manoeuvres by Louis XII, whose object was to force the Venetians from the high ground into the plain, the French vanguard found itself unexpectedly near to the rearguard of the enemy. A dry river-bed, sunk between steep banks, alone separated the two forces. Trivulzio and Amboise, who were commanding the French vanguard, at once opened fire with guns posted along the top of the bank on their side of the river-bed; at the same time their men-at-arms charged the enemy. Alviano, commanding the Venetian rearguard, sent for help to the Venetian commander-in-chief, replied to the French artillery fire with guns posted along his bank of the river, and with his infantry, protected by the

[1] Grumello, *Cronaca*, cap. xxxv; Porto, *Lettere Storiche*, nos. 11–16; Bembo, *Istoria Viniziana*, bk. vii; Mocenico, *La guerra di Cambrai*, bk. i; Guicciardini, *Istoria d' Italia*, bk. vii; Prato, *De rebus mediolanensibus*, pp. 272 *seq.*; Arluno, *De bello veneto*, bk. ii; Seyssel, *La victoire...[à]...Aignadel*, and Champier, *Le triomphe du très-chrestien Roy* (both in Godefroy, *Histoire de Louis XII*); Marillac, *Vie du connétable de Bourbon*.

steep bank and surrounding vineyards, repulsed the first charge of the French cavalry. At this point the resemblance to the battle of Fornovo ceases. Alviano, receiving orders from the Venetian commander to break off the fight and to follow the main body, chose nevertheless to continue to resist the French, while Trivulzio and Amboise, undismayed by the first check, bombarded the enemy ceaselessly and fed the attack with the fresh troops which continued to arrive. As the numerical odds increased against the Venetians they were compelled to abandon their favourable ground for more open country. There they were defeated by troops of the French main body.

This battle is a good example of correct action by an advance guard. It is the duty of an advance guard which comes into contact with the enemy to strike at once. However inferior in numbers it may be when it joins battle, the continual arrival of fresh reserves will always rectify any momentary set-back due to bold action in the beginning. Trivulzio was right in engaging without delay, and the reward of his tactical insight was the destruction of the hostile rearguard and the retreat of the Venetian army. Alviano, on the other hand, was guilty of an error of judgment. As a rearguard commander his duty was to hold the enemy till he had induced him to deploy, and thus to check the rate of his pursuit, but not to continue a fight against ever-increasing numbers, while his own chances of support grew more and more remote. Still less was he justified in fighting on after receiving orders to break off the action. His capture was the penalty of tactical blundering. Another point to notice is that the French artillery, though not manoeuvred after the opening of the action, was able to render effective support to the attacks of the infantry and cavalry. Further, the prompt following up of the initial success by Louis XII—an unusual proceeding in a French commander—resulted in the conquest within fifteen days of the whole of the Venetian territory assigned to him by the League of Cambrai[1].

Ravenna (1512).

At Ravenna[2] we again find the opposing armies separated by a river. The army of the Holy League occupied an entrenched camp with the river Ronco on its left. Its front, which met the river at right angles on the left, gradually curved back towards the right. Progress in tactical skill is shown by the fact that the attacking force no longer contemplates an offensive across the bed of the river. Gaston de Foix crossed the river at a spot below the position of his adversaries and advanced frontally against them. The League troops were organized in depth—vanguard in front, main body immediately behind, and rearguard behind the main body. With the river on their left and entrenchments in front and on the right this battle-order was well fitted for defensive

[1] Guicciardini, *Istoria d' Italia*, bk. VIII.

[2] Floranges, *Mémoires*, bk. I; Loyal Serviteur, *Histoire de Bayart*, ch. LIV; Porto, *Lettere Storiche*, no. 66; Coccinius, *De bellis italicis*; Guicciardini, *Istoria d' Italia*, bk. X; Giovio, *Vita Marchionis Piscariae*, bk. I. For a fuller bibliography and a more detailed consideration of the battle see Appendix B, § 8, and Appendix A.

tactics. The formation in which the French advanced after their passage of the river showed that they on their side had matured a sound plan of attack. Their vanguard, consisting of infantry and cavalry, and their main body, with the exception of its heavy cavalry, moved forward in line on a wide front and enveloped the enemy on his right flank. Immediately behind this front line the cavalry of the main body lay in close support. The rearguard was left at the river crossing in general reserve. Both armies placed their artillery in front, and the battle opened with a prolonged mutual bombardment. In the course of this bombardment a part of the French artillery was manoeuvred in a way which decided the issue. The duke of Ferrara's guns were brought round to the right flank and rear of the hostile position, while other guns were taken back across the river and posted at a spot on the opposite bank from which they could command the enemy's left. The fire from these guns became so unendurable to the cavalry of the League that it was forced to leave the camp and to meet the French in the open. This move precipitated a general action. The Spanish and Italian infantry were constrained to follow in support of their cavalry, but when once the army of the League decided to accept battle outside the camp, their entrenchments and their defensive formation turned from a protection to an impediment. The vanguard and main body issued piecemeal and in some disorder into a battlefield which was enclosed in front and on the right by the vast sweep of the French line. Converging charges from this perimeter first broke the Spanish and Italian cavalry and then compelled the retirement of the Spanish infantry. The rearguard of the League fled from the field, and a final charge by some French men-at-arms from across the river forced an entrance into the camp and captured the remnant of its garrison.

The many contemporary writers who have left us records of this famous battle were impressed chiefly by the obstinacy of the struggle, by the unparalleled casualties, and by the decisiveness of the result. It is still more important as a landmark in the history of tactics. The encircling movement of the attacking force and the organization of the defence in depth, both show a grasp of tactical principle considerably above the average warfare of the period. Machiavelli acutely points out that the failure of the army of the League was due less to faulty tactics than to faulty engineering[1]. Their choice of ground and their protective works were not equal to defending them from the skilful gunnery of the enemy, and an enforced transition from defensive to offensive action placed them at an irremediable disadvantage in the subsequent hand-to-hand fighting. The converging charges of the French men-at-arms, the calling up of the reserve to complete the discomfiture of the opposing infantry, the pursuit of the enemy from the field, and the final capture of their camp—each of these phases of the fight contributed to the final victory—each was a limb of a well-knit organic

[1] *Discorsi*, bk. II, ch. XVII.

whole, and a proof that soldiers were at last learning the importance of co-ordinating arms and units. The failure of the invincible Spanish foot to maintain the fight when their supporting cavalry had been broken served yet further to impress on military opinion the interdependence of the different parts of an army.

Novara (1513) : *Marignano* (1515).

The battles of Novara and Marignano, considered together, exhibit both the scope and the limitations of the Swiss tactical method. Each of these engagements took the form of an attack by an army consisting, for all practical purposes, of infantry only on an army composed of infantry, cavalry, and artillery. On both occasions the Swiss employed their characteristic tactic of a multiple offensive by bodies of troops of uniform organization, but the result was in the one case complete victory and in the other case complete disaster. This reversal of fortune was due not to a deterioration in their own method but to an improvement in that of their opponents.

At Novara[1] the French were encamped in a position which was badly chosen and inadequately entrenched. Their cavalry was hampered in its evolutions by a marsh, and cut off from the infantry by canals and ditches. In their method of attack the Swiss showed great ability. One section made a detour and attacked the French in rear. A second section—the main body

[1] Floranges, *Mémoires*, bk. i; Du Bellay, *Mémoires*, bk. i; Giovio, *Istorie*, bk. xii; Guicciardini, *Istoria d' Italia*, bk. xi; Mocenico, *La guerra di Cambrai*, bk. v.

—advanced under cover of the crops and assaulted the French artillery, which was placed in the forefront of the army and guarded by German infantry. By skilfully synchronizing these two attacks the Swiss divided the attention of the French. While the battle was raging for the possession of the artillery a third section of the Swiss army advanced unperceived by crawling along the ground and, adding their weight to the contest, turned the scale against the Germans. Since the unfavourable terrain prevented the French men-at-arms from reaching the scene of this reverse, the loss of the guns meant victory for the Swiss. The French were driven from the field by the fire of their own artillery, and if the Swiss had possessed cavalry the retreat would in all likelihood have become a rout.

At Marignano[1] the Swiss repeated the tactics of Novara, but the errors of the French were not repeated. The army of King Francis was drawn up with the vanguard in a forward position on the right, the main body a bow-shot to their rear, and the rearguard behind the main body. Each "battle" consisted of all arms and the whole force was posted in a wide entrenched space which allowed all except the vanguard ample freedom for manoeuvre. The Swiss advanced in three bodies and joined battle with the French vanguard just before sunset. Owing to its restricted and exposed position the vanguard

[1] Francis I, Letter to the duchesse d'Angoulesme; Floranges, *Mémoires*, bk. I; Du Bellay, *Mémoires*, bk. I; Barrillon, *Journal*, ch. I; Guicciardini, *Istoria d' Italia*, bk. XII; Giovio, *Istorie*, bk. XV; Marillac, *Vie du connétable de Bourbon*; Prato, *De rebus mediolanensibus*; Vegius, *Ephemerides*, bk. I.

was giving ground when King Francis advanced with the main body, and by flanking fire from his guns and flank charges with his men-at-arms kept the Swiss hotly engaged till nightfall. During the night he withdrew his army to a position further back and re-organized it as one line with the vanguard on the right, the main body in the centre, and the rearguard on the left. At dawn the Swiss developed simultaneous attacks against the right front and the left flank of the enemy. Their third body they posted with their few guns opposite the French centre and assigned to it the dual rôle of a containing force and a general reserve. Once more King Francis met the attacks with a vigorous combination of cavalry shock action and frontal and flanking fire from guns, arquebuses, and crossbows; his German infantry remained unbroken and the guns they guarded uncaptured. When the Venetian allies of the French began to appear on the field, and when their own reserves had been launched in vain, the Swiss lost heart and retreated.

Marignano proved to the world that an army of infantry only, however bravely it may fight, is bound to fail before a skilful combination of infantry, cavalry, and artillery. At Novara the French succumbed to their own imbecility. At Marignano they adapted themselves to the shifting circumstances of the battle and improvised new remedies as new perils arose. Co-operation was the note of the French tactics, but it was not so much co-operation between "battles" as co-operation between arms. The combined action of the Swiss infantry battalions was no match for the combined action of the horse, the foot, and the guns of the French king. Ravenna had indicated, and Marignano proved, that the organization of an army according to its arms corresponded more with the realities of fighting than the division into "battles." The division into "battles" was not abandoned, but from this time forward its significance was administrative rather than tactical.

Bicocca (1522).

At the battle of Bicocca[1] a French army was again confronted with the problem of Ravenna. The imperial army was drawn up in a large entrenched camp protected in front by a sunken road and on the flanks and rear by ditches and streams. Artillery and infantry lined the embankment of the sunken road, cavalry occupied the central space of the camp, while a Milanese force of mounted and unmounted troops guarded a bridge which gave entrance into the rear of the position. Lautrec, the French commander, planned a multiple offensive. After a preliminary bombardment his Swiss infantry were to assault the camp frontally. A mixed force of infantry and cavalry was detailed for the simultaneous forcing of the bridge. He himself, with a body of men-at-arms, hoped to gain entrance to the camp by the ruse of wearing the imperial badge. The formation of a small

---

[1] Du Bellay, *Mémoires*, bk. II; Guicciardini, *Istoria d' Italia*, bk. XIV; Giovio, *Vita Marchionis Piscariae*, bk. II; Vegius, *Ephemerides*, bk. I.

local reserve and a large general reserve completed
his arrangements. The scheme was wrecked by lack
of co-ordination. The Swiss, who would not wait for
the French artillery to get into action or for the
proper development of the subsidiary attacks, were
repulsed by the arquebuses and muskets of Pescara's
carefully trained infantry; their retreat meant the
failure of the French effort.

It is doubtful, however, whether the most meticu-
lous co-ordination would have forced the imperial
position. Pescara, who had fought on the losing side
at Ravenna, turned to account the lessons of that
action when he withstood the French at Bicocca.
His earthworks in 1522 were as much superior to
those of 1512 as was the volume of his musketry fire
to that of Pedro Navarro's famous wagons filled with
arquebuses. It is worthy of note that Navarro was
in the French service at Bicocca and was therefore
able to experience the efficiency of a scheme of defence which he had tried unsuccessfully to bring to
perfection ten years before.

Pavia (1525).

When in 1525 the marquis of Pescara advanced
against the French who were besieging Pavia[1] he
found their main force encamped in a large walled
park adjoining the city. His object was to compel
them to action, or, failing that, to join hands with

[1] Du Bellay, *Mémoires*, bk. II; Passero, *Giornali*, pp. 316
seq.; Guicciardini, *Istoria d' Italia*, bk. xv; Giovio, *Vita Marchionis Piscariae*, bk. vi; Merula, *Chronicon*, bk. iii.

the garrison of Pavia by gaining possession of Mirabello, situated at a distance of two miles inside the
park. With this object he breached the wall of the
park under cover of darkness and sent forward the
marquis del Vasto with a force of infantry and cavalry
to attack Mirabello. At dawn he himself followed
with the remainder of the army. The route to Mirabello lay roughly parallel to the French front and
was lined all the way with French guns. Vasto
reached and captured Mirabello but the remainder
of the army was subjected as it marched first to a
violent bombardment from the hostile artillery on
its left flank and finally to a general attack by the
French army. Leaving a reserve in his entrenched
camp, King Francis advanced with his massed formations of infantry and cavalry drawn up in one line
and preceded by his artillery. The imperial army at
once faced to the left, with the result that the two
lines of battle stood front to front. In their eagerness
to reach the enemy the French men-at-arms deserted
their infantry and masked their guns, and this
blunder was the imperialists' opportunity. The different
sections of the French army were defeated in detail.
After an initial success the French cavalry were
broken and scattered by the new skirmishing tactics
of the light infantry hastily pushed forward by
Pescara. Vasto advanced from Mirabello and broke
the French left. The Swiss infantry, finding itself unsupported, fled from the field. The imperial landsknechts routed the infantry of the French centre and
the French reserves as they hurried to the rescue.

The capture of the king and a sortie by the garrison of Pavia completed the discomfiture of the royal army.

The victory of Pescara at Pavia was not due to consummate generalship. He owed his success partly to the mistakes of his adversary but more especially to his own audacity, which sprang from his confidence in the superior fighting power of his army. The French justified his daring by playing into his hands. Lack of co-operation between arms dissipated the French effort and gave the imperialists an excellent chance to employ their new combination of fire and shock tactics. The Swiss, who had so often scorned the assistance of other arms, were on this day particularly ineffective when robbed of cavalry support. This fact, and the mutual support rendered by the imperial cavalry and infantry, must have convinced even the unprogressive highlanders of the value of reciprocity in battle. The imperial artillery played an inconspicuous part in the fight, but all deficiencies were supplied by the new combination of shock and fire action. By the careful dovetailing of the tactics of musketeers, pikemen, and cavalry the marquis of Pescara had wrought for himself a new weapon. This weapon, first tested at the Sesia, was in 1525 still his exclusive possession. At Pavia it gave him an advantage similar to that which the needle-gun gave to the Prussians at Sadowa.

CHAPTER VII

FORTIFICATION AND SIEGECRAFT

IN 1494 the Italians were behind the rest of the world in the arts of fortification and siegecraft; thirty years later military engineers from northern Europe were visiting Italy in order to learn the latest achievements of their profession. In this branch of warfare more than in any other the Italians became the recognized teachers of their neighbours. Then as now they were pre-eminent in solving the problems of engineering, and this pre-eminence was attested by the spread throughout Europe, as a result of the wars we are discussing, of the "old Italian" style of fortification. Once again we see the Italian first adopting the practices of the barbarian and then improving and reapplying them.

The chief military characteristic of the twelfth, thirteenth, and fourteenth centuries was the triumph of defensive methods over offensive methods[1]. The fortresses of those days withstood the most powerful siege weapons known to man. Blockade was the only sure means of reducing a mediaeval stronghold, and blockade required a length of service of which mediaeval armies were seldom capable. With the invention of gunpowder the days of the impregnable fortress were numbered. By the middle of the fifteenth century guns had been invented which were

[1] Oman, *Art of War in the Middle Ages*, pp. 551–3.

capable of battering down the strongest walls. These
guns were in the siege train of Charles VII of France,
and with their aid he drove the English from his
kingdom. While Italian castellans were still able to
mock besiegers from their hilltops the French in a
single year reduced every castle in Normandy. At
the end of the century the big guns of the French
opened the way to Naples and showed the world by
a spectacular demonstration that existing methods of
fortification were obsolete. Walls which had hitherto
resisted long sieges now fell within a few days. The
artillery of the defence was unable to prevent the
French guns from pushing up quickly to within forty
paces of the ditch. Under cover of gabions or of
trenches or of the fire of smaller pieces the French
gunners got their heavy artillery into position in the
space of twenty-four hours. An even shorter period
was usually required for the breaching of the walls
and the successful launching of the assaulting infantry. Not only were the French in advance of their
neighbours in the practice of siegecraft but they had
also found the key to the new difficulties with which
they confronted the defence. In France was first
discovered the value of revetted earthworks as a
quick and effective reply to the unexpected violence
of the new siege weapons. The breaching of the
masonry walls could not be prevented, but it was
found that the subsequent assault on the breach
could be held up by means of a deep ditch dug on
the inside of the threatened section and backed by
a high earthen rampart. While the rampart served

as a platform for artillery and smaller arms firing frontally at the breach, there were built within the ditch smaller covered works of differing design and variously named (*e.g.* bastardeaux, moineaux, caponnières, capannati, casemates)[1] from which the ditch was swept by lateral fire. Flanking fire was also developed from large semicircular buttresses of revetted earth which were usually built at each end of such defences[2].

From this brief indication of the state of French siegecraft and fortification in 1494 it will be seen that the hope of the besieger centred in the big gun and the hope of the besieged in fronting and flanking earthworks thrown up for the occasion. In reducing the problem to these elements the French were ahead of their neighbours. The Italians had realized the defensive merits of trenches and ramparts when they recaptured Otranto from the Turks in 1481[3], but there had been no subsequent wars of sufficient importance to stimulate them to further experiments in this direction. The walls of the cities and citadels which Charles VIII's artillery reduced to ruins were usually protected by a ditch and strengthened by towers built into them at intervals, but little provision was made for the closing of a breach either by flanking fire or by opposing fresh obstacles. However, the one campaign of 1494–5 was sufficient to

[1] See Jähns, *Handbuch*, pp. 1154 *seq.*

[2] These methods of fortification and siegecraft are described by Philippe duc de Clèves, *Instruction de toutes les manieres de guerroyer*, bk. I, pp. 45 *seq.* and 85 *seq.*

[3] Guicciardini, *Istoria d' Italia*, bk. xv.

bring Italian military engineering abreast of the French. In a few brief months the Italian mind had assimilated the new lessons. The Italians who defended themselves against the duke of Orleans at Rapallo in 1494 sought to supply the deficiency of a wall by the hasty digging of a ditch and the raising of a barrier of beams and trestles. Their subsequent tactics were as primitive as their defences. Deeming it dishonourable to protect themselves by artifice, they threw down the barriers and advanced against the enemy only to be signally defeated[1]. We have already seen that the defenders of the fortresses of Naples were so convinced of the inadequacy of their defences that they surrendered to Charles VIII without awaiting the final assault[2]. The conduct of the sieges which destroyed the French power in Italy is in marked contrast to this mixture of ignorance and pusillanimity. The besiegers of Novara in 1495 fully understood the necessity of entrenching themselves. Large bands of labourers were hired to assist in digging carefully mapped trenches. The artillery was pushed up to the walls under the protection of gabions and ramparts. Trenches were dug for the defence of the outlying districts of the city as they were successively brought into the power of the besiegers[3]. When Guillaume de Villeneuve was besieged in Trani in the same year he was hemmed in

[1] Giovio, *Istorie*, bk. I; Senarega, *De rebus genuensibus*, p. 541.
[2] See pp. 90, 94–5 above.
[3] Benedetti, *Il fatto d' arme del Tarro*, bk. II. Cf. also Sanuto, *La spedizione di Carlo VIII*, bk. IV.

by a continuous trench which abutted in each direction on the seashore[1]. A similar trench, which effectively prevented the approach of relief, was dug by King Ferdinand during his siege of the fortresses of Naples[2]. A Neapolitan who was in charge of a band of labourers engaged in these digging operations tells us how his men were pushed forward at each successful assault in order that the ground gained might quickly be put into a state of defence[3]. This siege is famous moreover for the employment of a new device of siegecraft—the explosive mine. From very early times walls had been ruined by the digging away of their foundations. As the earth and masonry were excavated so wooden props were inserted to prevent a premature collapse. Inflammable materials were introduced and ignited when the time was ripe for the assault, and with the burning of the props the wall fell in. The inclusion of gunpowder among the inflammable materials, said to have been done first by the Genoese at the siege of Serezanello in 1487[4], opened men's eyes to the possibility of removing walls violently from their position instead of merely converting them from a rigid obstacle to a scarcely less formidable heap of ruins. In 1495 the explosive mine was not yet brought to perfection. An inadequate charge of powder produced a collapse rather than a violent removal of the wall of the Castel Nuovo

---

[1] Villeneuve, *Mémoires*, p. 273.
[2] Guicciardini, *Istoria d' Italia*, bk. II.
[3] Guarino, *Diario*, 27 Nov. 1495; and cf. Giovio, *Istorie*, bk. III.
[4] Guicciardini, *Istoria d' Italia*, bk. VI.

at Naples. Nevertheless its partially explosive character is attested by eyewitnesses[1], as is also the fact that its author was an Italian[2]. Italy is already beginning to teach rather than to learn.

The years which intervened between the expedition of Charles VIII and the opening of the war against Venice in 1509 were years of experiment for the military engineers of Italy. King Charles had shaken their faith in the protective properties of masonry. They therefore began to explore the defensive possibilities of the trench, the rampart, and the flanking earthwork, and the offensive possibilities of the mine and the big gun. For fourteen years these methods competed with each other in local Italian wars; the result of the competition was seen when Italy became once more the theatre of a European struggle. The long contest between Florence and Pisa is an object lesson in the increasing power of the defence. The direct teaching of the French allies of Pisa is traceable at Pontesacco in 1495 where the Florentines were held up by a trench dug along the inside of the wall[3]. In the same year we find the Pisans defending their city with a trench half a mile long and the Florentines making local assaults and "digging in" on the ground gained[4]. In 1499 they

---

[1] *E.g.* Villeneuve, *Mémoires*, p. 283 (in Michaud et Poujoulat, Nouvelle collection, 1st Ser. vol. IV); Passero, *Giornali*, p. 89. Giovio, who was not present, exaggerates its explosive character (*Istorie*, bk. III).

[2] "Un capitano nominato lo signore Loise de Capua, valent' uomo," according to Passero, *loc. cit.*; Giovio attributes it to a certain Narcisso Toscano.

[3] Giovio, *Istorie*, bk. III.   [4] *Ibid.*

opposed Gian Paolo Vitelli by means of a deep ditch, furnished with casemates, dug in rear of the breach: behind it they raised a high rampart on which much artillery was mounted[1]. By these methods the Pisan citizens kept Vitelli at bay despite his counter-works dug by multitudes of hired labourers, and in the following year they were equally successful against the veteran troops of France[2]. The French king was surprised and angered, while the Florentines, in their humiliation, seized and beheaded the unfortunate Vitelli. It is a mistake to class this very drastic act of vengeance with the many political murders of the period. The execution of Vitelli was a military rather than a political or personal event. It showed that Italians, with the expedition of Charles VIII fresh in the memory, refused to admit that the failure of a siege could any longer be excused on military grounds.

Meanwhile the other cities of Italy were busily employed in improving their defences. In 1496 the duke of Ferrara began to dig a new ditch flanked

[1] Guicciardini, *Istoria d' Italia*, bk. IV. A Pisan citizen has also left us a description of this work, which is more detailed than that of the Florentine writers: "Stimasi era lungo braccia mille o più; una pertica cinque braccia. Era di grossessa da piè braccia diciotto, in cima braccia quattordici. Era d' altessa col suo parapetto, ch' era grosso braccia cinque, elto di verso le mura braccia venti in circa, con un gran fosso di verso le mura, e alsì di verso San Paullo, in modo era immesso a due fossi largissimi e fondi; ed era discosto el riparo dalle mura circa braccia dodici" (Portoveneri, *Memoriale*, 1 Aug. 1499).

[2] The defences which withstood the French were an improvement on those which withstood Vitelli. They included "un bastione grossissimo...con molte casematte sotto, con bombardiera per ogni parte; el quale è inespugnabile cosa" (Portoveneri, *Memoriale*, 14 Aug. 1500).

with large towers and to build new walls round his capital, and so anxious was he to complete the work that it was continued even on Sundays[1]. In 1499 King Ferdinand began the new fortifications at Naples amid the enthusiasm of his subjects[2]. When in this same year Cesare Borgia marched against Forlì, Caterina Sforza, the virile mother of Giovanni de' Medici, showed her appreciation of the recent achievements of siege artillery by flooding the surrounding country and denuding it of all natural cover[3]. Subsequently Borgia was held up at the siege of Faenza by a ditch and a rampart[4], and when in 1503 he found he could make no headway against the obstinate citizens of Ceri he employed a new siege engine as high as the town walls and capable of holding 300 fighting men[5]. The monster proved useless, its inventor was killed in the course of its erection, and Ceri was eventually reduced by the moral effect of a prolonged and violent bombardment, but the eagerness with which commanders adopted new devices serves to illustrate the experimental character of the siegecraft of these years[6].

[1] *Diario Ferrarese*, 10 May and 10 Aug. 1496.

[2] *Cronica Anonima*, 1 Nov. 1499.

[3] Priuli, *De bello gallico*.

[4] Guicciardini, *Istoria d' Italia*, bk. v.

[5] Giustinian, *Dispacci* 313 and 332.

[6] It is interesting to note in this connexion that in 1507, instead of an old-fashioned joust, there was organized at Milan in honour of Louis XII a sham attack on an artificial bastion, which was flanked by trenches and guarded by two towers at its two front corners each capable of holding from 25 to 30 men. It was designed by Charles d'Amboise and is described by D'Auton, *Chroniques de Louis XII*, 1506-7, ch. xxxiv.

The explosive mine was now brought to perfection by Pedro Navarro. To this interesting personage, who began his career as a private soldier and who lived to be the most trusted military adviser first of Spain and then of France, military engineering owes a debt similar to that which strategy and tactics owe to the marquis of Pescara. Both were animated by the same enterprising and experimental spirit. Both represented on the military side the intellectual audacity, the freedom from the bonds of tradition and routine, which characterized the Italian Renaissance. As the lieutenant of the Great Captain Navarro had recently been earning enduring fame in the war against the infidel. At the siege of Cephalonia in 1500 he had blown the first mine which was predominantly explosive in character[1]. In 1503 he introduced this new contrivance into western warfare by mining the Castel Nuovo and the Castel dell' Uovo at Naples. The detailed descriptions of these mines which are given by writers of that age, the moral effect of the unparalleled explosions to which they gave rise, and the speedy surrender of the unhappy French garrisons exposed to their terrors, would prove their novelty if it were not also vouched for by the actual words of contemporary historians[2]. It is curious to note that the explosive mine has changed little since its first introduction. Both in

[1] Giovio, *Vita Consalvi Cordubae*, bk. I.

[2] Guicciardini, *Istoria d' Italia*, bk. VI; cf. Giustinian, *Dispaccio* 419. Buonaccorsi, *Diario*, p. 75, does not mention the mine but he thinks it cosa maravigliosa that so strong a fortress should have been taken so soon.

the essential principles of their design and in the exceptional amount of slow, painful, and continuous labour which they require there is little difference between the mines of Pedro Navarro and those which have recently pitted the departments of north-eastern France.

Pisa continued to resist Florence until the year 1510. Earthworks proved now as potent a protection as in their day had been the mediaeval castles, and in the one case as in the other famine alone could reduce the garrison. A systematic cutting off of supplies both by land and sea eventually reduced a city which had been continuously inferior to its conquerors in military strength. Florentine writers attributed the prolonged resistance of the Pisans to the strength of their walls or to the peculiarly gluti-nous character of the earth with which they made their ramparts[1], but the true reason was the out-stripping of offensive by defensive methods and a reversal of the relation between siegecraft and forti-fication which had been set up by Charles VIII's triumphal campaign. The condition of apparent stalemate to which siege warfare was thus reduced reflected itself in the military opinion of the day. It gave rise to a controversy with which later genera-tions have not been unfamiliar. There were those who contended that under the new conditions men were of less importance than guns, that in modern warfare artillery was no longer an auxiliary but the

[1] Cf. Machiavelli, *Arte della guerra*, bk. VII; Guicciardini, *Istoria d' Italia*, bk. IV.

principal arm. There were others who defended the traditional view that in the last resort military decisions will always be achieved not by the action of mechanical contrivances but by human bodies directed by human brains[1]. The unsettled opinions of those in authority are further illustrated by the action of Guido Ubaldo, duke of Urbino, who on returning to his dominions after the fall of Cesare Borgia caused all the existing fortresses to be dismantled[2].

When the League of Cambrai went to war with Venice in 1509 the debate was transferred to a European arena. From the outset both sides showed that they were sensible of the progress which had been made in methods of fortification. Louis XII took the field accompanied by great numbers of labourers[3]. Alviano.prepared for a possible siege of Vicenza by devastating its neighbourhood[4]. After the disaster of Agnadello, however, the courage of the Venetians for a time failed them. City after city surrendered to the invaders without even a show of resistance. Then the unpreparedness of the emperor Maximilian gave the Republic fresh courage. Padua, which had surrendered its keys to the emissaries of the emperor, returned to the allegiance of St Mark, and here the Venetian government resolved to resist the titular chief of Christendom. The siege of Padua was a real trial of strength between the defensive and offensive tactics of the day. Each side had ample

---

[1] Cf. Machiavelli, *Discorsi*, bk. II, ch. XVII.
[2] *Ibid.* bk. II, ch. XXIV.
[3] Guicciardini, *Istoria d' Italia*, bk. VIII.
[4] Porto, *Lettere Storiche*, no. 5.

time to make elaborate preparations. Maximilian
collected the most formidable siege train of that
generation[1]. Venice gave the defence of the city into
the hands of the commander-in-chief Pitigliano, and
sent thither the sons of her noblest houses. Inventors
flocked to Pitigliano to press the claims of new
engines of war. Thoroughness marked the measures
of defence. Houses close to the walls of the city were
destroyed. The deep exterior ditch was filled with
water. All gates and weak points were guarded by
flanking artillery mounted upon bastions projecting
from the city wall. The wall was reinforced with a
continuous earthen embankment built against its
inner face. Behind this was a ditch thirty feet wide
having sheer sides revetted with masonry and containing casemates and towers at intervals of a hundred paces. Behind this again was another embankment, with a high protecting parapet, which served
as an assembly place for troops and as a platform for
artillery. The city was divided for purposes of defence
into quarters: each subordinate commander was
allotted a special section of the wall for which
he was made personally responsible, and a general
reserve of troops was kept for emergencies. Against
such preparations Maximilian was powerless. Al-

---

[1] Buonaccorsi gives the strength of Maximilian's force as
follows: 14,000 landsknechts, 4000 venturieri of different
countries, 6000 Spanish infantry, 3000 Italian infantry, 2000
cavalli sui proprii, 4000 cavalli Borgognoni, 1600 French
lances, 700 mandatigli in suo favore dal Christianissimo, 200
Papal lances, 250 lances from the duke of Ferrara, 600 Italian
lances under various condottieri, and about 200 pieces of
artillery tra grosse e piccole (*Diario*, p. 143).

though he at first pushed forward his advanced troops to the edge of the ditch without having recourse to sapping, he was soon forced, by the violence of the artillery fire from the city, to dig trenches for all arms. Although he threw down long stretches of the wall, the deep water in the ditch prevented him from either mining or assaulting with success. After immense efforts his storming troops gained a footing on one of the bastions only to be driven off again by an immediate counterattack. The raising of the siege marked a turning-point in the history of fortification. A system of defence had been evolved which could baffle a siege train many times more formidable than that of Charles VIII[1].

The lessons of this memorable siege were extensively applied during the years which immediately followed. Towns were everywhere defended on similar lines. In the first place the neighbouring country was devastated in all directions[2]. Then the ditch and the

[1] For the siege of Padua 1509 see Guicciardini, *Istoria d' Italia*, bk. VIII; Bembo, *Istoria Viniziana*, bk. IX; Mocenico, *La guerra di Cambrai*, bk. II; Porto, *Lettere Storiche*, nos. 27–31; Cordo, *La obsidione di Padua*; Loyal Serviteur, *Histoire de Bayart*, chh. XXXIII–XXXIV; Buonaccorsi, *Diario*, pp. 143 *seq.* Maximilian, in his letter of 7 Oct. 1509 (Le Glay, *Correspondance de l'empereur Maximilien*, vol. I, p. 190), is quite candid as to the chief reason for his failure: " considéré le grant nombre d'artillerie et de gens de deffence que les Vénitiens y avoient et mesmement les grandes réparations qu'ils y avoyent faictes, que jamais au monde n'a esté veu les semblables...il nous estoit plus prouffitable de délaisser icellui assault que de le donner."

[2] Or flooded if practicable; *e.g.* the Venetians made use of extensive floodings in the winter campaign of 1509–10: the French took Legnago because they succeeded in stopping up the holes made by the Venetians in the embankment of the Adige (see Mocenico, *La guerra di Cambrai*, bk. III).

existing wall were backed either directly or at a short distance with trenches and ramparts. An instance of the rapidity with which such works could be raised is provided by Bourbon's defences at Milan in 1516. In forty-eight hours he built a huge terraced embankment which contained pikes on the lower level in front, small arms on a higher level in the middle, and artillery on the highest level in rear[1]. The final and most important precaution of all was the construction of strong points which could command the walls and the ditch from the flanks. Gun-chambers, casemates, and similar works were erected on the floor or in the sides of the ditch, while above ground there were built out from the walls projecting earthworks from which guns could rake the rampart, the walls, the ditch, and the surrounding country[2]. To these latter works, which were usually semicircular in shape, the general term "bastion" came to be more particularly applied. It was found that carefully sited bastions could forbid ingress to a town even when the wall had been breached and the ditch crossed. Notable instances of the efficacy of the bastion in defence are the repulse of Foix from Ravenna in

[1] Marillac, *Vie du connétable de Bourbon*, p. 162.
[2] Bembo, describing the defences of Trivigi in 1511 (*Istoria Viniziana*, bk. x, p. 279), gives a good summary of the state of fortification in that year: "le mura rifaceva; delle Torri quelle che per antiqua usanza più alte erano, che la presente ragion d' arte militare non ricerca, la parte di sopra ne levava: le fosse più alte e più larghe faceva: ingrandiva gli argini: fuori della città per mezzo miglio le case a terra gittava: gli alberi tagliava, sicchè nulla cosa o alla vista, o alle palle delle artiglierie, che si traessero, fare impedimento potesse."

1512[1] and of the French and Venetians from Verona in 1516[2]. On both these occasions Marcantonio Colonna was in charge of the defence.

While defenders of towns continued thus to apply and to develop the methods employed at Padua, besiegers had the harder task of discovering how to counter them. The most pressing problem—the protection of the besieging army in devastated country and against continuously active artillery—was solved by an extension of the system of trenches and gabions. The army encamped out of gunshot range and then slowly and laboriously sapped forward with its artillery by means of zigzag trenches. The first example of such systematic sapping was the siege of Padua by the viceroy of Naples and Prospero Colonna in 1513. The siege failed for the significant reason that, although they employed great numbers of labourers, they were nevertheless unable to hire sufficient for their purpose[3]. When Navarro besieged the citadel of Milan in 1515 he protected his operations with deep trenches and with ramparts made of sand and brushwood which varied in height from fourteen to twenty-four feet[4]. At the siege of Mondolfo in 1517 Lorenzo de' Medici, owing to his neglect of such precautions,

[1] Giovio, *Vita Leonis X*, bk. II.

[2] Guicciardini, *Istoria d' Italia*, bk. XII.

[3] *Ibid.* bk. XI. Yet only two years before Pedro Navarro, when besieging the Ferrarese fortress called by Bembo the Bastita, had been able to sap forward to the edge of the ditch in three days (Bembo, *Istoria Viniziana*, bk. XII, p. 307). This illustrates the rapid progress of the defensive in these years.

[4] Giovio, *Istorie*, bk. XV.

lost eight bombardiers within one hour[1]. When siege-guns had been pushed forward to within effective range of the walls, one of two methods was employed, during these central years of the Italian wars, in order to render the defences assailable by the storming troops. Either a torrent of projectiles was concentrated on one particular spot, or an attempt was made to create and to keep open several gaps at the same time. Although the heavy guns of the duke of Ferrara which reduced Legnago in 1510 are said by Paolo Giovio to have overcome the resistance of stone, timber, earth, and brushwood[2], nevertheless there is hardly a single subsequent case of the defences of a town being rendered untenable by bombardment alone. On the other hand a besieging commander occasionally succeeded by dividing the attention of the garrison between several breaches. In 1516 the French and Venetians bombarded the walls of Brescia in five different places. The garrison, which numbered only 700, was unequal to the double strain of resistance and repair, and succumbed eventually to a fivefold assault[3]. When later in the year the same two armies laid siege to Verona, Lautrec, the French commander, breached the defences in five places and left such short lengths of wall standing between the gaps that he was able to enfilade the defenders who were constructing works behind the ruins. Despite superhuman exertions on the part of

---

[1] Guicciardini, *Istoria d' Italia*, bk. XIII.

[2] Giovio, *Vita Alfonsi Ferrariae*.

[3] Giovio, *Istorie*, bk. XVI.

the besiegers, however, the town was still holding
out when the approach of relief compelled the abandonment of the siege[1].

One result of the very qualified success of prolonged and violent bombardments was an increase
of mining[2]. With a single explosion a mine might
remove defences which had defied the efforts of the
heaviest guns. As soon as Pedro Navarro appeared
in northern Italy with the Spanish army in 1511 he
became the terror of garrisons. So redoubtable was
his reputation that when in 1515 he undertook the
mining of the citadel of Milan, a virgin fortress reputed the strongest in the world, the mere knowledge of his operations terrorized the Swiss defenders
into capitulation[3]. Other garrisons, however, were
less inclined to yield tamely to these methods.
Countermining was practised and received a new
importance. In earlier days those who countermined
had aimed at meeting the original mine and stopping
its progress by subterranean combat. Now the object
was rather to dig air-passages into the hostile mine
and thus to break the force of the eventual explosion.
A device such as this so weakened Navarro's mine at
Bologna in 1511 that the ruined wall subsided into
its former place[4]. Further successful countermining
against Pedro Navarro was carried out at Brescia in

[1] Giovio, *Istorie*, bk. XVIII.

[2] D'Auton, *Chroniques de Louis XII*, 1506–7, ch. XXIV, notes
that there were 200 mineurs attached to the French artillery
train for the expedition against Genoa in 1507.

[3] Giovio, *Istorie*, bk. XV; Floranges, *Mémoires*, bk. I; Du
Bellay, *Mémoires*, bk. I; Barrillon, *Journal*, ch. I.

[4] Porto, *Lettere Storiche*, no. 61.

1516[1]. Various devices were used for the detection of mining operations: Philippe de Clèves recommended the suspension of needles over basins of water[2]; at Bologna the right spot was discovered from the sound vibrations of bells and rattles placed on drums along the walls[3]. From this time onwards mine and countermine became an accompaniment of nearly all first-class sieges. Such operations were sometimes prevented when the outer ditch was dug deep and filled with water. This indeed became the only important argument for a wet ditch as against a dry ditch, since, from the point of view of the besieger, the difficulties of damming or draining a wet ditch were counterbalanced by the absence of casemates to interfere with the actual crossing[4].

The new system of fortification which had been evolved under the stress of the earlier campaigns was widely adopted by the cities of Italy during the five years of peace which followed the treaty of Noyon. In the *Chronicle of Cremona* we have evidence of the kind of work which was being everywhere pushed forward[5]. Cremona, which in 1516 remained in the hands of the French, was the scene of almost continuous building. The ditch was enlarged, the walls were terraced, and bastions and strong towers were erected. With the resumption of fighting in 1521 the

---

[1] Giovio, *Istorie*, bk. XVI.   [2] *Instruction*, bk. I.

[3] Porto, *Lettere Storiche*, no. 61.

[4] Cf. the discussion of this subject in the Discurs of Joannis Thomae von Venedig, quoted in Zetter, *Kriegs und Archeley Kunst*, ch. CXIII.

[5] *Cronache Cremonesi* 1494–1525.

work was prosecuted with even greater energy. The countryside was levelled, further bastions were built to guard the gates and the citadel, and when at last the war reached Cremona, the multitudes of peasants employed as labourers by both sides (and paid out of the pockets of the unfortunate Cremonese) were forced to work in places where artillery fire caused them numerous casualties. The same increased interest in fortification is traceable in the military writings of these years. Machiavelli had argued in 1513 that a ruler who possesses a strong army can do without fortresses[1]. In the *Art of War*, written in 1520, this contention no longer appears. On the contrary he deals in detail with the design of fortresses and advocates angular walls, a double ditch, a rampart, and towers and casemates at frequent intervals. He decides against projecting bastions on the ground that they are too exposed to the converging attacks of the enemy[2]. On this subject the practical soldier, della Valle, writing in the following year, shows more insight than Machiavelli. Bastions, he says, have the double advantage over walls that they are more quickly built and less susceptible to artillery fire[3].

During the last decade of the Italian wars soldiers were more occupied with questions of fortification and siegecraft than with any other branch of their profession. The character of these concluding campaigns

[1] *Discorsi*, bk. II, ch. XXIV.
[2] *Arte della guerra*, bk. VI.
[3] Vallo, *Libro continente appertenentie ad capitanii*, bk. I, ch. VII.

was governed by the prevailing addiction to the methods of siege warfare. Commanders were less inclined than in the years immediately preceding to run the risks of open fighting, and often preferred to shelter themselves behind the walls of a fortified city or the ramparts of an entrenched camp. The reliance on earthworks rather than masonry as a protection against heavy artillery induced an approximation between the methods of permanent fortification and of field defences. In both cases the trench, the rampart, and the bastion were the mainstay of the defence, and an attack on an entrenched camp, as at Bicocca and Pavia, differed in no essential particular from the storming of a fortress. It was a period of trench warfare in which the spade played as important a part as the musket. Nevertheless it was in these very years that the lessons of defence which had been painfully learnt at the cannon's mouth began at last to be translated into permanent masonry. The period of fluctuation in opinion, which found its most convenient expression in works of earth and timber, gave place to an era of dogmatic teaching and structural fixity. We have now briefly to consider first the efficacy of the new system as illustrated by the sieges of these later years, and then the distinctive characteristics which make it recognizable as a definite style of fortification.

The value of the new system of defence is proved by the comparative rarity of successful sieges between the years 1521 and 1528. On the few occasions when an important fortress was taken, the result was due almost invariably either to the skilful use by the besiegers of favouring circumstances, as when the marquis of Pescara took Genoa in 1522, or to moral weakness on the part of the defence, as when Milan fell to the imperialists in 1521. When attack and defence were fairly pitted one against the other, and each side made use of all the resources it could command, then the defence either triumphed completely or succumbed only after a long struggle. A good instance of an impregnable defensive system is provided by the famous lines with which in 1521 Prospero Colonna guarded the citadel of Milan. They were designed to prevent the relief of the garrison which was beleaguered in the fortress and were regarded by contemporaries as the finest military work of the age[1]. Two parallel crescent-shaped trenches were dug over a distance of one mile. Each was backed by a continuous rampart and between them a roadway was left, twenty paces in breadth, on which infantry, cavalry, and artillery could move in formation. Strong bastions which supplied lateral gunfire were built at each end, while smaller ones were distributed at intervals along the entire length. Pedro Navarro carefully reconnoitred these works with a view to attacking them, but after much trench-digging and mining he was compelled at last by the hopelessness of the outlook to abandon the undertaking. A trench of equal length and with a similar purpose was designed by Lautrec and Navarro when

[1] Described by Guicciardini, *Istoria d' Italia*, bk. XIV, and Giovio, *Vita Marchionis Piscariae*, bk. II.

they besieged Naples in 1528[1]. In this case, however, sickness delayed the work, with the result that sorties by the garrison were able to pierce the line and to block communication between the French army and the Venetian fleet. The investing force was thus reduced to the condition of a beleaguered garrison, and one more example was added to the long list of unsuccessful sieges.

Examples of successful sieges are perhaps even more illustrative of the power of the defence. In laying siege to Cremona in 1527, the duke of Urbino, who was in command of the Venetian army, avowedly relied on spades rather than on arms. His efforts were directed chiefly against one bastion. Sapping up to the bastion, he dug beneath it an assembly trench from which he intended to launch his assaulting troops. The defenders on their side dug trenches to protect the bastion, and, issuing from these trenches, attacked and captured the Venetian assembly trench. After much fighting the disputed trench was evacuated in the end by both sides. The duke of Urbino now sapped further forward and dug five new trenches with a view to launching an attack not on the bastion but on the trenches guarding the bastion. This new

---

[1] Guicciardini, *Istoria d' Italia*, bk. xix. These lines, like those of Prospero Colonna at Milan, earned the admiration of the world, and especially of the imperialists when they eventually occupied them. Segni says of them: "i quali a giudizio universale degl' ingegni militari...furono tenuti eccellentissimamente fatti, come quegli che erano così ordinati da Pietro Navarro, sopra ogn' altro capitano illustre, peritissimo delle fortificazioni, e nell' espugnazioni delle terre, e nel maneggio dell' artiglieria" (*Storie Fiorentine*, bk. ii).

attack was successful, the enemy was driven back
on to a longer line and eventually came to terms[1].
The same method of concentrating the attack on one
bastion and preparing for the assault by the digging
of assembly trenches was practised with success by
the French and Venetian armies against Pavia in
1528. Here the preliminary bombardment wrought
such havoc, and the main attack was so skilfully
supported by demonstrations against other parts of
the wall, that the storming troops, who advanced in
three waves, were able after two hours' bitter fighting
to carry the breach and reduce the city[2]. There is
little difference between siege warfare such as this
and the technically open warfare which led up to the
battle of Pavia. The imperial army approached the
fortified camp of Francis I by sapping, by entrenching,
and by building bastions and strong points. Eighteen
days were consumed in this warfare of spades before
the marquis of Pescara deemed the time ripe for the
great decision[3]. In the history of the Italian wars,
the Pavia campaign marks the nearest approach between the methods of permanent fortification and
those of field defence. The influence of antiquity
and the impetuosity of the Swiss had produced increased elaboration in the construction of entrenched
camps[4]. Ditch and rampart, bastions and flanking
guns, are all laid down by Machiavelli as necessary

[1] Guicciardini, *Istoria d' Italia*, bk. XVII.
[2] *Ibid.* bk. XIX.
[3] *Ibid.* bk. XV.
[4] See Oman, *Art of War in the Middle Ages* (Lothian Essay),
p. 92.

for the safety of an army's temporary halting-place[1]. After Pavia the two classes of protective work begin to draw apart once more. Camps continue to be strongly fortified, but town defences, now that they are approaching uniformity of design, cease to be built of temporary materials. Stone, which the guns of Charles VIII had made unpopular, once more comes into use in the building of permanent fortresses.

This return to more substantial building was inevitable. Italian castles had fallen before Charles VIII's artillery not because they were made of masonry but because they were ill-designed to resist the new siege engines. The resisting power of fortresses, which are immovable, will always tend to exceed the destructive power of siege guns, which are limited by the necessity of being movable. But at certain times in the history of warfare the development of siege weapons has outstripped the development of fortification. At such times fortification becomes fluid. The defending side has recourse to experiment and improvisation with the materials which are always at hand, namely earth and wood. When a new type of defence, capable of supporting the new conditions, has been evolved, fortification becomes once more rigid and uniform and embodies itself in more durable materials. A crisis of this kind occurred in Italy at the end of the fifteenth century. The ramparts and bastions which figure so largely in the subsequent campaigns were tentative efforts to solve the new problem of defence.

---

[1] *Arte della guerra*, bk. VI.

They resemble the clay model which precedes the marble statue. When the model gave satisfaction it found expression in a more enduring medium. The new stone fortresses which arose out of the Italian wars were the work of Italian architects who were on this subject the teachers of Europe. Michele Sanmicheli (1484–1559) and Sangallo the younger (died 1546) translated the provisional earthworks into terms of masonry. The essence of the new style—the "old Italian" style as it is now called—was the bastion. The supreme importance of lateral and diagonal fire from projecting bastions was the discovery of the Italian wars. Bastions started as semicircular earthen buttresses and ended as massive polygons of stone. They replaced the old mediaeval towers along the perimeter of fortified towns, and supported each other with their guns along the intervening stretches of wall ("the curtain"). Stone was also used for all the minor features of the new style of fortification— for the revetting of the ditch and the rampart, for the casemates, for the gun-platforms, and for the cavalieri.

The spread of the new style of fortification was necessarily slow. The poverty of Italian cities during the sixteenth century led to a perpetuation or adaptation of existing defences more often than to the erection of entirely new works. The first town to be fortified on the "bastioned trace" was Verona in the third decade of the sixteenth century. Sanmicheli supervised the work. During the same decade the defences of Parma, Piacenza, and Ancona were reorganized on the same plan by Sanmicheli and Sangallo[1]. Within a few years Albrecht Dürer was embodying the new ideas in the fortresses of the Low Countries. Thirty years before this Martini had included among numerous suggested designs for fortresses certain plans which somewhat resemble the bastioned trace. On the strength of these plans he has been acclaimed by some as the originator of the old Italian system of fortification[2]. It must not be forgotten, however, that the value of projecting works for the development of flanking fire had long been recognized. Vegetius, writing in the fourth century, had recommended angular walls with towers at the angles[3]. Moreover there is no evidence that Martini's plans were ever put into execution or that

[1] Pedro Navarro was also an authority on the new style of fortification, although, unlike Sanmicheli and Sangallo, his name did not become associated with particular works. In 1526 he accompanied Machiavelli in an inspection of the walls of Florence and advised many alterations, among which should be noted (a) a continuous ditch: "in ogni luogo dove sono mura si faccia fossi, perchè dice quelli essere le prime difese delle terre." (b) The exclusion of a borgo which was overlooked by high ground. (c) The lowering of the towers and their replacement by casemates, round baluardetti, or full-sized baluardi, i.e. bastions. (d) The erection of mutually supporting baluardi where the walls formed angles and flanking the gates, "secondo che oggì si usano fare forti" (Relazione di una visita fatta da N. Machiavelli per fortificare Firenze, in Opere, vol. VI, p. 352). Many of these recommendations were carried out, Sangallo being responsible for the design of the bastions. The Florentine public was indignant at the destruction of the mediaeval towers (see Varchi, Storia Fiorentina, bk. II, § 21).

[2] Martini, Trattato di architettura civile e militare (ed. Carlo Promis): see especially Plates XXXIII and XXXV and the editor's commentary on the former.

[3] De re militari, bk. IV, ch. II.

he attached more importance to them than to the many less practical plans which accompany them. Sanmicheli, on the other hand, built the earliest bastion, in the modern sense of the word, of which we have knowledge. To him, therefore, if to any single individual, is due the honour of originating a type of fortification which was to bring fame to Vauban and to influence military engineering as late as the nineteenth century[1].

[1] This view of the origin of the bastion is in accord with that of Jähns, *Handbuch*, pp. 1154 *seq.*, and *Geschichte des Kriegswissenschaft*, pp. 282 *seq.*, 438, 792. I have also consulted Zanotto, *Le fabbriche civili, ecclesiastiche, e militari di Michele Sanmicheli*. For an early example of the bastioned trace see Map II.

CHAPTER VIII

MILITARY WRITERS

THE Italian Renaissance was the beginning of a new era for military thought. The same process of expansion and specialization which has been remarked in dealing with military practice is observable also in the development of military theory. Before the Renaissance heralded the dawn of the modern age the only kind of literature which was devoted to the art of war in the abstract was the military text-book. The ancient world had produced many collections of rules for the guidance of commanders. Some, like the *De stratagematis* of Frontinus, consisted merely of illustrative examples culled from the warfare of the past; others, like the more famous *De re militari* of Flavius Vegetius, were text-books in the modern sense of the term—collections of general precepts and particular instructions for the waging of war. The Middle Ages had accepted such books as authoritative and had failed to improve upon them.

With the invention of gunpowder, however, an element was introduced into warfare which was not treated in the ancient text-books. Consequently for this new subject special treatises came to be written, and, since the subject was in its infancy, there was continual need for a revision or a supplementing of the accepted views. A sense of progression was thus introduced into military studies, and the way prepared for the arrival of a truly scientific spirit. That spirit was supplied by the Italian Renaissance. In Italy first arose the scientific treatise dedicated to the arts of war. With the beginning of inquiry into the mechanical laws governing the firing of guns and the building of fortresses there began the separation, so marked in our own day, between the learned arms and the less technical branches of soldiering. That was the first important specialization which occurred in military studies at this time. Another, equally important, arose more directly out of the wars which we have been considering. Machiavelli, in the course of his inquiries into the nature and functions of the State, was drawn to consider the relations between warfare and politics. He is the first secular writer to attempt to allot to the practice of arms its place among the collective activities of mankind, to define its aims, to regard it as a means to an end. With Machiavelli war ceases to be accepted as an isolated phenomenon recurring at intervals throughout human history. He was not a soldier by profession and took no interest in the practice of war for war's sake. He was the first of the long line of writers who take a philosophical survey of the art of war, who study it with a view not so much to surprising the secret of victory as to assessing the possibilities and the limitations of armed force. Whereas the writer of the military text-book expounds the facts of war as he finds them, and whereas the scientific inquirer seeks from a minute study of the practice of the present to devise improvements for use in the future, the

political philosopher, taking human society as his
theme and all time as his province, attempts to
establish general rules for the universal guidance of
military effort.

This triple branching of military studies into works
of instruction, of research, and of abstract synthesis,
is the contribution of the Italian Renaissance to the
theoretical side of the art of war. It involved a
recognition of the interdependence of the different
branches of human knowledge. The soldier began to
profit by the labours of the philosopher and the
savant. Nevertheless the text-book, written by
soldiers for soldiers, remained then, as it remains
to-day, the commonest form of military writing.
With the increase of profane learning in the fifteenth
century manuals of military instruction had become
more numerous and better written. Several such
manuals now appeared in Italy as a result of the
Italian wars. The ablest of these was a treatise published by Philippe duc de Clèves in 1498 entitled
*Description de la forme et la manière de conduire le
faict de la guerre*[1]. Although the writer was a commander in the French army, the fact that he saw
service in Italy and that he became in 1499 governor
of Genoa gives him a claim to mention among Italian
military writers. He is interesting to the student of
military history because he describes in detail the
art of war as it was practised by the French during
the earlier Italian campaigns. His book belong more

---

[1] It was republished under other titles, *e.g.* that cited in
these notes.

to the modern world than to the Middle Ages. War
is no longer an adventure but a complicated, responsible, and prosaic business. He has only very rare
traces of mediaevalism, as, for instance, when he
says that if a commander win a "bataille assignée"
he must remain three days on the field, but if the
action be a "grosse rencontre" he need remain on the
field only for the following night[1]; or, again, when
he implies that it is hardly a reputable form of warfare to shut oneself up in a town and submit to a
siege[2]. Except for such occasional remarks as these
the book is a precise and exhaustive account of contemporary warfare. He describes minutely the French
system of attack on fortresses—the rapid pushing
forward of the guns by means of trenches, gabions,
and covering fire[3]. He describes also the current
system of fortification with inner ditch and rampart,
casemates and "demi-ronds"—the germ of the
bastion—and insists on pioneers and gunners working
in close association[4]. He recommends the orthodox
battle formation of the day—massed pikes bordered
by light infantry with missile weapons, supported by
cavalry on the wings and artillery in front[5]. The
most valuable part of his treatise, however, consists
of general advice, the ripe fruit of his own wide
experience. He insists throughout on the necessity
for constant precaution, on the avoidance of risks,
on protection by means of energetic entrenching and

---

[1] Philippe de Clèves, *Instruction de toutes les manieres de
guerroyer*, pt. I, p. 84.
[2] *Ibid.* pt. I, p. 86.   [3] *Ibid.* pt. I, pp. 45 *seq.*
[4] *Ibid.* pt. I, pp. 21, 44–5.   [5] *Ibid.* pt. I, pp. 74 *seq.*

vigilant sentries[1]. He recognizes the advantage, though not the absolute necessity, of a reserve in battle[2]. Commanders, he says, should on all occasions give personal supervision and encouragement to their men: "I advise you often to mount a horse and to ride round the camp; in that way you will see if it is well protected and fortified, and also your men will be pleased to see you, and you will be in consequence so much the more loved and feared[3]." There are probably few junior officers who have not at one time or another received some such advice as this from their military superiors. Philippe de Clèves further shows his practical outlook by emphasizing the responsibility of subordinate commanders, the importance of keeping a roster of duties, and the necessity of accurate topographical information. Soldiering for him is a matter of patient arrangement and careful administration. He has none of the spirit of the knight-errant. He is more akin to the modern staff-officer.

It will be well here to consider for a moment the increased attention which was now being paid by soldiers to geography. In urging the importance of topographical information Philippe de Clèves was reflecting the opinion of his time. The cultivation of an eye for country, reconnaissance before action, the utilization of natural features in battle, and attention to climatic and meteorological changes were not only

---

[1] Philippe de Clèves, *Instruction de toutes les manieres de guerroyer*, pt. I, pp. 45 *seq.*
[2] *Ibid.* pt. I, p. 82. [3] *Ibid.* pt. I, p. 38.

recommended by military writers but were practised by soldiers and encouraged by governments. Maps were more frequently used and became more detailed and accurate[1]. In 1518 Francis I celebrated the marriage of Lorenzo de' Medici with a sham attack on a sham village flanked by sham woods[2]—a development of the mediaeval joust which affords a striking proof of the increased attention to natural features in warfare. The Venetian ambassador, Marco Foscari, who was sent to Florence in 1527, furnished his government with a detailed and very able analysis of the strategic situation of Tuscany, in which he examined carefully the military value of the roads into the Florentine state, and the accessability of the capital[3]. When Sanmicheli was appointed in 1513 by the Venetian Republic to supervise the fortifications of Udine with a view to preventing the invasion of Friuli, he sent to the doge a masterly report urging that the mere strengthening of a single town was not enough to hold up an invader, that the mountain frontier and the sea coast, of which he described the salient geographical features, should be further surveyed and guarded by fortresses, and that the main defensive line should be drawn along the difficult valley of the river Livenza. When it is remembered that Sanmicheli was a professional builder

---

[1] *E.g.* the map used by the besiegers of Novara in 1495 showed the city, roads, marshes, woods, rivers, ditches, and villages (Benedetti, *Il fatto d' arme del Tarro*, bk. II, p. 39).

[2] Floranges, *Mémoires*, bk. I, p. 225.

[3] *Relazioni of the Venetian Ambassadors*, Series II, vol. I, pp. 7 *seq.*

of fortresses, this report of his, which insists on the superior defensive value of natural barriers, is seen to be a tribute both to his own breadth of view and to that Italian power of envisaging large problems as a whole which was reshaping the mind of Europe[1].

A military text-book hardly inferior in influence to that of Philippe de Clèves was published in 1521 by Giambattista della Valle di Venafro[2]. It is the work of an active soldier who served under the duke of Urbino and who wrote avowedly as a practical man and not as a theorist. He treats everything in minute detail and thoroughly represents the phase of development reached by the art of war at that time. He fully realizes, for example, the importance of the infantry arm. He advocates the cultivation of the military spirit among the footsoldiery and bases it on smartness in externals—care and cleanliness in dress, marching in step, movement to the sound of the drum[3]. He complains that the proportion of infantry equipped with firearms is never high enough[4]. For the defence of towns he recommends deep ditches, casemates, ramparts, bastions, and an energetic employment of lateral fire[5]. In siege work he realizes the importance of adequately entrenching men and guns and of digging zigzag communication

[1] This report, *Discorso circa il fortificar la città di Udine*, is in *Arch. Stor. It.*, Nuova Serie, vol. XIV.

[2] *El perfeto capitan* and other titles; usually known as "Vallo."

[3] Vallo, *Libro continente appertenentie ad capitanii*, 1524, bk. II, ch. XXV.

[4] *Ibid.* bk. II, ch. XV.

[5] *Ibid.* bk. I, ch. V.

trenches[1]. Occasionally he shows himself in advance
of the average military thought of his time, as, for
instance, when he says that formation in battle is
of less importance than mobility—the capacity to
thrust out a wing at the right moment and to develop
a flank attack[2]. At other times the old Adam of
chivalric warfare appears, as when he prefers hand-
to-hand fighting to stratagem in battle[3]. In many
ways della Valle illustrates better than any other
writer the outlook of the soldiers who fought in Italy
between the years 1494 and 1529. His book is ill-
proportioned and over-burdened with detail; he de-
votes a whole book to the etiquette of duelling; he
does not realize, as do Machiavelli and Guicciardini,
that he is living in a time of transition in military
methods. Nevertheless all the latest developments
in the art of war find a place in his book and fighting
as he describes it has something of the character of a
vast experiment. Both his defects and his merits are
characteristic of a period when the art of war was
in the melting-pot. He gives equal weight to old
practices which are soon to be discarded and to new
practices which will in time revolutionize the profession of arms. Gifted civilians may, from a detached standpoint, attempt to analyse contemporary
warfare and to forecast its future. Della Valle is
content to describe facts as he finds them, and the
result is the truest picture we have of soldiering

[1] Vallo, *Libro continente appertenentie ad capitanii*, 1524,
bk. II, ch. I.
[2] *Ibid.* bk. II, ch. XLII.
[3] *Ibid.* bk. I, ch. X.

in Italy in the first quarter of the sixteenth century.

Before passing to more learned works mention should be made of an essay on siegecraft and fortification written in 1525 by Joannes Thomae[1] of Venice. The essay survives only as a fragment embedded in a later book and presented in the German tongue[2]. Nothing is known of the writer except that he was obviously an experienced soldier. The sole importance of the few pages of instruction is the additional evidence they afford of the progress of defensive warfare. The task of the defenders is given as a twofold one—keeping the enemy at a distance and throwing him back if he comes near. For these purposes the commander of a besieged city is exhorted to destroy all cover in the neighbourhood, to build a double earthen rampart protected by a deep ditch, and to be so discreet that his intentions shall be hidden both from the enemy and from his own soldiers. The truly practical character of Joannes is shown by his insistence on a large stock not only of food and munitions but also of money for the payment of the troops.

Of the many Italian savants who in this period turned their attention to problems of war two have left important contributions to military literature.

---

[1] *I.e.* John the son of Thomas.

[2] "Ein Discurs Joannis Thomae von Venedig weylandt Keyser Caroli V nachmals der Herzschafft zu Venedig fürtrefflichen Ingeniers von Beschützung und Eroberung der Vestungen und anderer Kriegssachen mehr," forming ch. cxiii in Zetter, *Kriegs und Archeley Kunst,* 1619.

The *Trattato di architettura civile e militare* of Francesco di Giorgio Martini and the *Quesiti et inventioni* of Niccolò Tartaglia both deal, among other non-military matters, with the subjects of artillery and of fortification. For this reason, and also because the one book appeared at the opening and the other at the close of the Italian wars, Martini and Tartaglia may very profitably be considered together. Martini, architect and engineer, who was employed in works of fortification by Duke Federigo of Urbino, confines his treatment of the subject of firearms to an enumeration and brief description of the different types of gun, and to a statement of the ingredients of gunpowder[1]. There is no suggestion either of classification or of experiment. On the subject of fortification he is more progressive. He realized, at a time when Italy still relied on the mediaeval fortress, that bombardment was to be resisted less by the strength than by the plan of the walls[2]. Writing before the expedition of Charles VIII he suggested the adoption of a polygonal trace with round towers at each angle and with flanking defences at each gate[3]. The subsequent wars proved the efficacy of his general design. In 1538, nine years after the treaty of Cambrai, appeared Tartaglia's *Quesiti et inventioni*. Tartaglia was a mathematician. He boasts that his work is that of a man who has never fired a gun, or been engaged in building fortifications, and who believes "that the eye of the mind sees more deeply into general

[1] Martini, *Trattato*, bk. VII, chh. I and II.
[2] *Ibid.* bk. v, ch. IV.   [3] *Ibid.*

things than does the eye of the body into particulars[1]."
On the subject of gunnery he deals not only, like
Martini, with the composition of gunpowder[2], but
also with ballistics, with trajectories, and with the
rules of sighting[3]. On the subject of fortification he
repeats Martini's maxim that the strength of fortresses consists less in massiveness than in design,
and then, sifting the experience of a generation of
warfare, proceeds to describe a model fortress with
a saw-edged perimeter and with a strong three-
cornered bastion of stone at each inner and outer
angle[4]. With the aid of diagrams and giving mea-
surements he deals in turn with every detail of the
model fortress and claims for it many advantages,
of which the most important are that its walls cannot
be bombarded perpendicularly, that its curtain will
always be further removed from the enemy than its
bastions, and that its guns will be able to sweep
any assaulting party from four different directions[5].
This purely scientific treatment of the technical side
of warfare was a new phenomenon in the military
history of modern Europe. It meant that the art of
war had reached a stage of complexity at which it
required for its further progress the assistance of the
learned. The rise of firearms and the consequent
impetus which was given to fortification engendered
a new branch of the art of war, and the growth of
this branch depended on a systematic study of scien-

[1] Tartaglia, *Quesiti et inventioni*, bk. VI, qu. 8.
[2] *Ibid*. bk. III.   [3] *Ibid*. bk. VI, qu. I.
[4] *Ibid*. Gionta to bk. VI.   [5] *Ibid*. bk. VI, qu. 3–5.

tific laws. The mathematician therefore came to the aid of the soldier. Later the necessity for closer co-operation produced a class of soldier who was both a fighting man and a man of science, and to members of this class was entrusted the practice of gunnery and of military engineering. But the rise of the learned arms has not prevented the governments of modern Europe from having recourse in times of crisis to the older practice of utilizing civilian brains in the solution of military problems.

It remains to consider the greatest military writer of the period, Niccolò Machiavelli. Machiavelli was not a soldier, though as Secretary to the Ten he was closely associated with the formation of the Florentine militia. He was never present at any important engagement, though his embassies brought him into contact with high commanders and famous armies. In spite of his energetic military organizing and propaganda he was never interested primarily in the subject of war. His outlook was political rather than military, but, unlike the majority of his own and of succeeding generations, he recognized no opposition between those two terms. He conceived the civilian and the soldier not as two distinct persons with separate and often conflicting aims, but as the same man in two different aspects. It was the duty of the citizen to be also a soldier; soldiering was a branch of citizenship and warfare was a branch of politics. An army was a highly specialized department of the civil service. The direction of an army in the field was a part of the wider business of statecraft. This view was not peculiar to Machiavelli. It had been tacitly accepted and fully acted upon in the earlier ages of both the ancient and modern world. In the city-states of antiquity and in the semi-tribal states of the Dark Ages the army had been but the civil population under arms. With the gradual separation of functions which was a condition of the advance of civilization there arose in each case a professional military class. This led to a more intensive cultivation of the art of war, but it also led to a narrowing of the military outlook. War came to be practised for its own sake. A broader view of war had been taken by the citizen of the tribal state when summoned from his herds to slay the marauder or to pillage his neighbour. Though he did not formulate his conviction he knew that the ultimate aim of armed force was the good of the community. No such view was held by the commanders of mercenary bands who hawked their services about Italy in Machiavelli's time; nor did directors of national armies, in their efforts to attain particular objects, pause to analyse the more general motives which guided the employment of armed force. In undertaking this task, in once more linking up military action with political theory, in seeking once more to identify the soldier with the civilian, Machiavelli was preaching a new gospel to the rulers of Europe. In his own country his seed fell on stony ground, and among neighbouring peoples it at first brought forth little fruit, but if his direct influence was small he is assured of a permanent military significance as the spiritual ancestor of Grotius and the prophet of the citizen armies which Europe has subsequently improvised in her struggles to be free.

Those works of Machiavelli which deal in the abstract with military topics are *The Prince*, the *Discourses on the First Decade of Titus Livius*, and the *Seven Books of the Art of War*. The two former works, which were written before the year 1513, are concerned with war only as an accompaniment of political action: the *Art of War*, on the other hand, is a military text-book. Nevertheless all three works contain both general and particular maxims. Luminous advice for the guidance of belligerent powers may be embedded in a discussion on tactics. Consequently in order to appraise Machiavelli as a military writer it is necessary to classify his remarks on the art of war not according to the books in which they occur, but according to their scope and tendency—to consider him first as a teacher of the technicalities of fighting practised within the army, and then as the adviser of the government which is to direct its operations.

As a teacher of the details of soldiering Machiavelli employed keen powers of observation and a well-developed logical faculty, but he lacked the advantages of personal experience and of theoretic training. Consequently, though his argument is always stimulating, his conclusions are often mistaken. His treatment of each branch of the art of war, with two notable exceptions, betrays itself sooner or later as the work of a brilliant amateur.

On the subject of strategy, for instance, he recognizes
without hesitation the supreme importance of topographical knowledge[1] and the true value of diversion[2], but he is not thereby deterred from advocating
the abandonment of a mountain barrier to an advancing enemy for the sake of fighting in less restricted surroundings[3]. Again, he sees that the true
value of the Swiss echelon formation lies in its provision of a support and a reserve; nevertheless, when
he comes to embody this principle in an ideal battle-
order of his own, the example of ancient Rome leads
him to arrange his infantry in column[4]—a formation
inferior in offensive power to the Swiss echelon. He
is on firmer ground when he insists on implacable
pursuit after victory[5]—sound advice much needed
in his generation. As one would expect, Machiavelli
goes farthest astray on the more technical side of
warfare. He consistently depreciates the importance
of firearms. He is half inclined to banish artillery
from the battlefield altogether[6], and to arquebuses
he contemptuously assigns the rôle of overawing the
peasantry[7], as shot-guns are used to scare birds. In
1513, despite the recent example of Padua, he doubts
the wisdom of building fortresses at all[8]; in 1521 he
recognizes the more obvious of contemporary methods
of defending towns but fails to see that the bastion
is the keystone of the new system[9]. In contrast to
these academic half-truths is the insight and firm

[1] *Prince*, ch. XIV.   [2] *Arte della guerra*, bk. VI.
[3] *Discorsi*, bk. I, ch. XXIII.   [4] *Arte della guerra*, bk. III.
[5] *Ibid*. bk. IV.   [6] *Ibid*. bk. III.   [7] *Ibid*. bk. II.
[8] *Discorsi*, bk. II, p. 24.   [9] *Arte della guerra*, bk. VI.

grasp of reality which characterize his treatment of the subjects of infantry and cavalry. He abandons theorizing for the interpretation of actual experience. As Secretary to the Ten he had been engaged in raising the Florentine militia and shaping it for the war with Pisa, and the result of his contact with actuality is seen in the uniform correctness of his teaching. Cavalry he reduces unhesitatingly to the status of an auxiliary arm, defines accurately its special duties, and enumerates its limitations in comparison with infantry[1]. He maintains that the training of infantry should aim at inuring the men to hardship, making them expert in the use of arms, and accustoming them to act together[2]. The course of training should begin with instruction in assembling in battle-order quickly and smoothly, and should then proceed to collective drill, handling of arms, and movement by signal[3]. He insists moreover that the infantryman should be taught to dig and deprecates the clogging of the military machine by the employment of multitudes of hired non-combatant labourers[4]. Thus one touch of reality transforms Machiavelli's brilliant but untrustworthy theories into practical rules which still find a place in modern instructional manuals[5].

Machiavelli's fame as a military writer, however, rests not on his practical teaching but rather, as we have already indicated, on the soundness of his

---

[1] *Discorsi*, bk. II, ch. XVIII; *Arte della guerra*, bk. II.
[2] *Arte della guerra*, bk. II.   [3] *Ibid.* bk. III.
[4] *Ibid.* bk. V.   [5] Cf. *Infantry Training*, 1914, ch. I.

general principles. War, in his view, is the handmaid of politics, and on this doctrine as a foundation he rears a fabric of military wisdom knit together by copious citations from classical history and buttressed with many shrewd apophthegms of his own. His plea for the institution of a citizen army well illustrates the dynamic quality of his ideas. Money, he declares, is not the sinews of war, but good soldiers; good soldiers will readily get you gold, and the only sure way to get good soldiers is to train your own subjects[1]. Elsewhere he proclaims the principles which should underlie the training of the citizen army: "To insure an army being victorious in battle you must inspire it with the conviction that it is certain to prevail. The causes which give it this confidence are its being well armed and disciplined, and the soldiers knowing one another. These conditions are only to be found united in soldiers born and bred in the same country. It is likewise essential that the army should think so well of its captain as to trust implicitly to his prudence, which it will always do if it see him careful of its welfare, attentive to discipline, brave in battle and otherwise supporting well and honourably the dignity of his position[2]." The secret of good discipline, as he says in another place, is to pay well and punish well[3].

Having in sentences such as these, which are worth many pages of his opinions on more technical matters,

---

[1] *Discorsi*, bk. II, ch. X, and cf. bk. I, ch. XLIII.

[2] *Ibid.* bk. III, ch. XXXIII (trans. N. H. Thomson).

[3] *Arte della guerra*, bk. V.

sketched what may be called the soul of his ideal
army, he proceeds elsewhere to deal with the qualities required in its commander. His decision in this
matter has been confirmed by many masters of the
art of war. He requires in a commander first a good
knowledge of topography[1] and secondly a good intelligence system[2]. Energetic reconnaissance and
constant reference to the map will enable a commander to screen his own operations and at the same
time to discover those of his adversary. Of this
Machiavelli says, "in the whole art of war there is
nothing so useful[3]"; and again, "it is the highest
quality of a captain to be able to forestall the designs
of his adversary[4]." When he passes to the ultimate
question of the relations between the commander in
the field and the home government, Machiavelli,
though a civilian and a believer in the strict subordination of the military arm to the civil, shows nevertheless that he is alive to the dangers of a hampered
military command. He cites divided command as
one of the most active of the causes of the overthrow
of armies[5], and characterizes as mischievous the
Venetian and Florentine practice of interfering unduly with the conduct of leaders in the field[6]. These
observations are in no way inconsistent with his view
of the dependence of the commander on the prince.
He merely advises the prince to trust the expert
whom he has put in charge of the military depart-

[1] *Prince*, ch. XIV; *Discorsi*, bk. III, ch. XXXVII.
[2] *Arte della guerra*, bk. V.   [3] *Ibid.*
[4] *Discorsi*, bk. III, ch. XVIII.   [5] *Ibid.* ch. XV.
[6] *Ibid.* bk. II, ch. XXXIII.

ment of the public service. That he wishes the prince to maintain a constant supervision of the military arm—that he considers warfare indeed to be the most important concern of a ruler—is proved by his dictum that a prince should give his whole energies to the study of the art of war[1].

The bearing of this opinion on the political doctrine of Machiavelli is seen in the sentences which open Chapter XL of Book III of the *Discourses*: "Although in all other affairs it be hateful to use fraud, in the operations of war it is praiseworthy and glorious; so that he who gets the better of his enemy by fraud is as much extolled as he who prevails by force.... This, however, I desire to say, that I would not have it understood that any fraud is glorious which leads you to break your plighted word, or to depart from the covenants to which you have agreed; for though to do so may sometimes gain you territory and power, it can never, as I have said elsewhere, gain you glory.... The fraud, then, which I here speak of, is that employed against an enemy who places no trust in you, and is wholly directed to military operations[2]." The importance of these sentences lies less in their substance than in their tendency. Into a discussion of one important sphere of human activity Machiavelli will not allow the intrusion of ethics. Here we first glimpse the political standpoint from which he wrote *The Prince*. If the prince's chief business be war, and if war be freed from the ordinary restraints of

[1] *Prince*, ch. XIV.
[2] Trans. N. H. Thomson.

morality, then it is but a short step to the consideration of the other functions of the prince from a non-
moral point of view. In the *Discourses* Machiavelli
protests that it is only from warfare that he would
exclude ethics as irrelevant: in *The Prince* he makes
no protestation—he tacitly warns morality from the
threshold. There seems little doubt that Machiavelli's theoretical separation of statecraft from
morality was a direct outcome of his meditations on
the art of war. Fraud has always been acknowledged
as admissible in war. Machiavelli had but to picture
the rivalries of states as a continuous condition of
open or covert warfare, and he had reached the non-
moral standpoint from which he wrote *The Prince*.
The world never acknowledged the non-morality of
statecraft, and it is worth remembering that such a
claim was never specifically made by Machiavelli.
He merely approximated his political outlook to the
military outlook of the world in general, and it is
thus to the analysis by the Florentine secretary of
the principles of warfare that we must trace the
origin of the diplomacy of Frederick the Great and
of Talleyrand.

Reference has already been made to the frequency
with which Machiavelli supports his arguments with
references to antiquity. Both the *Discourses* and the
Art of War might be described as a plea for a return
to the military customs of the ancient world. The
Romans are taken as exemplars not only of military
teaching of universal validity, such as the cultivation
of the higher military virtues, but also of rules of

more particular application, such as the close formation of infantry, the secondary rôle of cavalry, and
the value of earthworks in fortification. Now the
fact that the greatest military writer of the age based
his recommendations on the authority of antiquity,
coupled with the fact that many of the actual changes
made in the art of war at this time were a transition
from mediaeval to ancient methods, points to the
conclusion that the ancient world directly influenced
the military development of modern Europe. There
is no doubt that the whole of Italian public life was
then influenced by classical study. How far that
influence in the military sphere shaped the development of military method, and how far it was merely
a superficial colouring of the military literature and
phraseology of the time, is a calculation very difficult
to make. Many commanders who fought in the
Italian wars were certainly well versed in polite
letters. Gian Giacopo Trivulzio was a classical
scholar who took a historical interest in his profession[1]. Antonio Giacomini is said to have cited
examples from ancient history in his military discourses to his subordinate commanders[2]. The schools
of the condottieri which characterized the soldiering
of the preceding century must have drawn precepts
from antiquity at a time when all teaching took a
classical orientation. But if we go further back to
the ages before the Renaissance we find that an aca-

---

[1] Cf. *Relazioni of the Venetian Ambassadors*, Series II, vol. v,
the dispatch from Milan, 1520.
[2] Pitti, *Vita di Antonio Giacomini*, p. 251.

demic interest had always been taken in the military doctrines of the ancient world. The authoritative military text-book of mediaeval times was the *De re militari* of Vegetius, a practical guide to the art of war written in the fourth century. That the influence of this work was considerable in the eleventh century is shown by the fact that Aegidius Romanus, who wrote one of the few military treatises of the Middle Ages, bases his teaching on Vegetius and acknowledges his indebtedness no less than nine times[1]. After the invention of printing Vegetius was one of the earliest authors to be multiplied in many tongues[2]. That his reputation was maintained at the height of the Renaissance is proved by his influence on Machiavelli. The Florentine secretary obviously wrote his *Art of War* with Vegetius at his elbow. He treats some subjects in a very similar manner[3], some of his phrases are unmistakable echoes from the *De re militari*, while the general rules at the end of the book follow those of Vegetius word for word and are presented in the same order except for one misplacement and one substitution[4]. Though Machiavelli is no slavish follower of Vegetius, and though

[1] Aegidius Romanus, *De regimine principum*, bk. III, pt. III: the references to Vegetius occur in chh. III, V, VI, VII (twice), VIII (twice), XII, and XX.

[2] Editions were published at Utrecht in 1473, at Ulm in 1475, at Rome in 1478, at Rome again in 1484, and at Erfurt in 1511 (Jähns, *Handbuch*, p. 815).

[3] Compare his treatment of fortification, *Arte della guerra*, bk. VII, with that of Vegetius, *De re militari*, bk. IV, especially the beginning.

[4] Compare Machiavelli, *Arte della guerra*, bk. VII (*ad fin.*) with Vegetius, *De re militari*, bk. III, ch. XXVI.

by employing similar methods of inquiry he often
reaches different conclusions, nevertheless his debt
to the author who had shaped the military thought
of the Middle Ages proves that, even on its literary
side, the development of the art of war in the early
sixteenth century was less of a break with the Middle
Ages than is generally supposed.

In the actual practice of the art of war at this time
it is hard to discover any indisputable outcome of
classical teaching. Tommaso Carafa, who commanded a Neapolitan force against the French in
the campaign of 1495–6, is said by Paolo Giovio to
have lost a battle by disposing his troops in the form
of a crescent, "according to the custom of the
ancients," and the historian adds that such imitation
of the ancients had often been the undoing of Italian
commanders[1]. The same writer implies that the lines
which Prospero Colonna dug for the defence of the
citadel of Milan were modelled on those which Julius
Caesar dug at Alesia[2], but it seems very probable
that Giovio was led to suggest this classical inspira-
tion by the obvious resemblance between the two
works. A more transparent instance of a historian
seeing studied imitation where there was only acci-
dental similarity is Merula's remark that Prospero
Colonna was indebted to Roman teaching for his
fortified camps and Fabian tactics[3]. As against such
very jejune evidence of classical influence in military

[1] *Istorie*, bk. III.
[2] *Vita Marchionis Piscariae*, bk. II.
[3] *Chronicon*, bk. I, p. 85.

operations we have to remember that the two greatest commanders of the age, Gonsalvo de Cordova and the marquis of Pescara, and the most famous of the younger generation of condottieri, Giovanni de' Medici, were all of them but indifferently trained in the humanities[1]. It should also be remembered that the branch of warfare which now developed to the greatest advantage of posterity—namely the use of firearms—was just that for which mankind owed no debt to antiquity. It therefore seems reasonable to conclude that there was little direct imitation of ancient practices. The influence of classical history and literature, like the influence of Vegetius in the Middle Ages, was mainly academic. We view the warfare of the Renaissance through the academic medium of contemporary historians and teachers and are consequently apt to form an exaggerated opinion of the effect of theoretical learning on military operations. Such an effect was undoubtedly produced, but it was indirect and incalculable. The revival of learning sharpened men's wits, widened their horizon, multiplied their interests. Italy, the home of the revival, overflowed with seminal ideas. Warfare, no less than other spheres of human activity, shared in the general revivification, but it remained like all the foremost concerns of modern Europe, the legitimate offspring of the Middle Ages.

[1] See Giovio, *Vita Consalvi Cordubae*, and *Vita Marchionis Piscariae*; Rossi, *Vita di Giovanni de' Medici*.

APPENDIX A

THE BATTLE OF RAVENNA

Movements preceding the battle.

THE immediate occasion of the battle of Ravenna was an attempt on the part of the army of the Holy League (consisting of Spanish and Papal troops) to force the French to raise the siege of the city from which the battle takes its name. Gaston de Foix, duc de Nemours, the French commander, was encamped on the south side of Ravenna between the rivers Montone and Ronco[1]. A small detachment of his army was on the western side of the city beyond the Montone, across which he had thrown a bridge. On Good Friday, the 9th of April, 1512, his storming troops had advanced from the camp to assault the breach made by his guns in the southern wall of Ravenna. The assault was unsuccessful. On the following day news reached Foix that the enemy was approaching from the direction of Forlì. Raymundo de Cardona, viceroy of Naples, the commander of the Spanish and Papal army, advanced along the right bank of the Ronco and halted north of Molinaccio, within two miles of Ravenna and within one mile of the French position[2]. Here his army spent the remainder of that Saturday and the ensuing night in

---

[1] See Map III. In 1512 these rivers flowed round Ravenna: in the years 1733–9 they were diverted to their present beds.

[2] See Note A, p. 205.

digging an entrenched camp. For Gaston de Foix, who was straitened for supplies, a speedy decision was a military necessity. The fact that the enemy had chosen to approach Ravenna along the right bank of the Ronco seemed to indicate an intention to relieve the city without coming into direct contact with the besiegers. The French captains therefore agreed to cross the Ronco on the following morning —that of Easter Day, the 11th of April 1512—and to compel the Spaniards to accept battle. The victory of Ravenna was the execution of this plan.

At dawn the French began to cross the Ronco about one mile below the Spanish position. A part of the army forded, since the river was everywhere fordable[1], and a part made use of a bridge of boats which had been built during the night. A force of 1000 infantry under Paris Scotto and 400 men-at-arms (the "rearguard") under Yves d'Alègre was left beyond the river to guard the camp and the Montone bridge and to hold in check the garrison of Ravenna. The remainder of the French army found itself, when it had crossed, in a low-lying plain free from trees and intersected by ditches[2]. Fabrizio Colonna, who was in command of the Spanish van-

[1] Floranges, *Mémoires*, vol. I, pp. 88 *seq.* (in the edition published by the Société de l'histoire de France). This reference will be shortened henceforward to "Floranges."

[2] Peter Martyr, *Opus Epistolarum*, no. CCCLXXXIII (referred to hereafter as "Peter Martyr"). Cf. also Bayard's letter of 14 April 1512, where he mentions grands fossés separating the French vanguard from the French "battle." (This letter is quoted in Appendix III of Roman's edition of the Loyal Serviteur, and will be referred to hereafter as "Bayard").

guard, wished to assault the French while they were engaged in crossing the river[1], but the viceroy, on the advice of Pedro Navarro, the leader of the Spanish infantry, contented himself with bombarding them from behind his defences[2]. When the French army had crossed the Ronco it wheeled to the right and, moving parallel with the river, advanced against the enemy.

Disposition of the opposing armies at the opening of the battle[3].

The French army advanced in line, with the cavalry on the wings. On the right wing, next to the river, were the men-at-arms of the vanguard (910 lances[4] commanded by Alfonso d'Este, duke of Ferrara, and Jacques de Chabannes, seigneur de la Palisse), and behind this force were the men-at-arms of the "battle" (780 lances commanded by Thomas

---

[1] Fabrizio Colonna, Letter quoted in Sanuto, *Diarii*, vol. xiv, col. 176 (hereafter referred to as "Colonna"); Guicciardini, *Istoria d' Italia*, bk. x (hereafter referred to as "Guicciardini"); Giovio, *Vita Leonis X*, bk. ii (hereafter referred to as "Giovio, *Leo X*"); Porto, *Lettere Storiche*, no. 66 (hereafter referred to as "Porto"); *Relacion de los sucesos de las armas de España...con la jornada de Rávena* (in *Coleccion de documentos ineditos para la historia de España*, vol. LXXIX, p. 274, and referred to hereafter as *Relacion*).

[2] Castello, *Depositione* quoted in Sanuto, *Diarii*, vol. xiv, col. 128 (hereafter referred to as "Castello").

[3] See Map IV. The only complete descriptions are those of Pandolfini (Letter in Desjardins, *Négociations diplomatiques de la France avec la Toscane*; referred to hereafter as "Pandolfini") and Guicciardini; other writers confirm them in many particulars.

[4] See Note B, p. 206.

Bohier, seneschal of Normandy[1]). On the extreme left of the line were 2000 light cavalry with about 1000 dismounted archers. Between these two masses of mounted troops marched three bodies of infantry: 9500 German landsknechts, commanded by Jacob Empser, on the right next to the men-at-arms; 8000 Gascon archers and Picard pikemen, commanded by the seigneur de Molart, in the centre; and 3900 Italians, commanded by Federigo da Bozzolo, on the left next to the light cavalry. To the men-at-arms of the "battle," posted behind those of the vanguard and therefore in rear of the general alignment[2], was assigned the rôle of a close support or local reserve. The general reserve, as we have seen, was the rearguard left at the river crossing. The artillery was drawn up in front of the French right. Foix did not attach himself to any particular unit, but exercised general supervision accompanied by a small troop of chosen men-at-arms.

The Spanish army was disposed in depth with the Ronco protecting its left flank. Like all the rivers of that part of Italy the Ronco is enclosed between embankments. In the sixteenth century these embankments were considerably lower than they are today, and, in the absence of a properly constructed road to Forlì, they served as the chief means of communication between that town and Ravenna. It was along the top of the embankment on the right of the river Ronco that the Spanish army had marched to its

---

[1] More accurately, "Général des finances de Normandie."
[2] See Note C, p. 207.

present position. The side of this embankment which
looked towards the river was steep, while that which
sloped down towards the land was skirted by a ditch.
The Spanish front, which was at right-angles to the
embankment, and the Spanish right flank were defended by a continuous trench[1]. Between the river
and the beginning of this trench a clear space of about
forty feet had been left, forming a narrow exit for
the cavalry. Within this fortified area were drawn
up, one behind the other, three bodies of heavy
cavalry: the vanguard (670 Papal lances commanded
by Fabrizio Colonna), the "battle" (565 lances commanded by the marquis della Padula, with whom
was the viceroy), and the rearguard (490 lances, the
"Company of the Great Captain," commanded by
Don Alfonso Carvajal). These cavalry units were
placed close to the river-embankment. The Spanish
infantry stood on the immediate right of the two
leading cavalry units, namely those of Colonna and
Padula. It was disposed in three divisions each of
which consisted of four coroneles or companies (a
coronela was between 500 and 600 strong). Between
the two rearmost of these divisions stood a separate
formation of 2000 Italian (Papal) infantry. Pedro
Navarro was in supreme command of the infantry.
The light cavalry, numbering about 1500 and commanded by the marquis of Pescara, was allotted the

---

[1] Coccinius, *De bellis italicis* (hereafter referred to as
"Coccinius") speaks of two ditches. The foremost of these
was probably not dug by the Spaniards: it was doubtless one
of the many ditches which drained the battlefield. *Relacion*
gives the depth of the Spanish trench as una brazia (= 6 feet?).

duties of a general support and was placed on the right of the infantry towards the rear of the position, but not so far back as Carvajal's rearguard, which stood behind all the other troops both mounted and unmounted[1]. The artillery, which was outnumbered by that of the enemy[2], was posted in front of Fabrizio Colonna's men-at-arms. In front of the infantry Navarro had drawn up a number of light carts containing arquebuses.

Navarro's carts[3].

These carts, of which the number, variously given by different writers, was not less than thirty[4], stood immediately behind that section of the trench which covered the front of the Spanish infantry. They were small, low, two-wheeled vehicles, built of light wood and capable of being propelled by the soldiers themselves. Upon them were mounted heavy arquebuses. The exact number of arquebuses placed on a single cart is uncertain, but, since the carts were small and the arquebuses of the heavier kind, the number can have been hardly more than two or three. From the

[1] For the foregoing description of the Spanish dispositions I have followed *Relacion* closely.

[2] By two pieces to one according to Colonna.

[3] Porto and Coccinius give the fullest descriptions of these carts. See Note D, p. 207.

[4] Guicciardini says 30, Pandolfini about 50, the letter quoted in Sanuto, *Diarii*, vol. xiv, col 126, about 70; Loyal Serviteur, *Histoire de Bayart*, ch. liv (referred to hereafter as "Loyal Serviteur") appears to say that there were 100. Buonaccorsi (*Diario*, pp. 170 *seq.*) and Nardi (*Istorie*, bk. v), who otherwise follow Pandolfini closely, agree with Guicciardini in giving the number as 30. Curiously enough none of the writers on the Spanish side refers to these carrette.

front of each cart protruded a sharp iron spear about six feet long. On each side of this—perhaps forming one piece with it—there jutted out curved iron blades shaped like scythes. From the back of each cart projected a wooden shaft six feet long which rested upon the ground when the cart was stationary and thus held it firm against an advancing enemy and also against any recoil produced by the discharge of the arquebuses. It thus seems to have answered very closely to the trail of a gun. It was also the means by which the cart was moved about.

The true significance of these carts cannot be appreciated unless it is realized that they were an infantry weapon. They were the invention of Pedro Navarro, the commander of the infantry, they were manned by the infantry, they were placed in front of the infantry. Their primary tactical function was undoubtedly that of a movable obstacle for the protection of the infantry, similar to the wagons used in the Hussite wars. As a movable obstacle they enabled a camp to be put quickly into a state of defence, but this protective rôle represented only half their usefulness. Their structural lightness shows that they were designed also for manoeuvre in the field. If they had been intended for stationary and defensive work only, a heavier four-wheeled wagon would have been more suitable. Those writers[1] are mistaken, however, who draw an analogy between

[1] *E.g.* Porto, Jacopo Guicciardini (Letter quoted in *Arch. Stor. It.*, Series I, vol. xv, pp. 307–19, referred to hereafter as "Jacopo Guicciardini").

the spears and blades of these carts and the scythes with which the war-chariots of the ancient world were sometimes fitted. The scythed chariots of Darius were designed for charging the enemy, whereas the spears and blades were the defensive side of Navarro's invention—a barrier against massed infantry and cavalry. The offensive value of the carts consisted in their extreme mobility and their armament of arquebuses. They represent an early attempt to solve the problem of manoeuvring heavy arquebuses in battle. This was, as we have seen[1], one of the most pressing military problems of the day. The weight of the heavy arquebus not only interfered with its rapid manipulation but also placed the arquebusier at a great disadvantage when at close quarters with troops equipped with the arme blanche. The problem was eventually solved by the adoption of the fork-shaped rest, and by the close association of the pikeman with the arquebusier in battle. Navarro's carts were a stage in the arrival of an effective combination of missile with shock action in infantry tactics. The carts themselves represent the part played later by the fork-shaped rest: the spears and scythes represent the pikemen and men-at-arms who protected and co-operated with Pescara's musketeers at the Sesia and at Pavia.

The preliminary bombardment.

The bombardment to which the French army was subjected during its passage of the river Ronco was

[1] Ch. III, p. 54 etc.

accurate enough to inflict casualties[1]. As soon, therefore, as the leading French troops, the infantry of
the vanguard, had crossed, Foix brought over his
guns and began at once to reply to the fire of the
Spaniards[2]. Under cover of this cannonade he now
passed across the remainder of the vanguard and the
"battle[3]," and, having deployed the combined force
in the manner described above, advanced to within
two hundred paces[4] of the Spanish camp. Here the
French army halted with its guns opposite the gap
in the Spanish defences[5] and with its left wing curled
slightly round the Spanish right[6]. In this position
the opposing forces remained for at least two hours[7],
and during that time there was developed the most
violent cannonade between armies in the field that
the world had yet seen. The losses on both sides
were very heavy[8]. In the early stages of the bom-

[1] Castello.

[2] Fino, Letter quoted in Tommasini, *Niccolò Machiavelli*,
vol. I, p. 706 (referred to hereafter as "Fino").

[3] *Ibid.*

[4] So Pandolfini; Guicciardini says 200 braccia, Jacopo
Guicciardini 2 bowshots, Floranges 2 stonethrows.

[5] Nardi, *Istorie della città di Firenze*, bk. v (referred to hereafter as "Nardi").

[6] Pandolfini, Guicciardini.

[7] Two hours according to Colonna, *Relacion*, Jacopo Guicciardini, Guicciardini, Coccinius, and the letter in Sanuto
XIV, 126; three hours according to Pandolfini, Floranges, and
Vignati (*Cronaca*, in *Arch. Stor. Lomb.*, 2nd Series, vol. I, p.
593, hereafter referred to as "Vignati").

[8] G. P. Silvestri, who visited the battlefield five days afterwards, says "sono venuti molti feriti più crudelmente ch' io
vedessi mai de le artelarie" (Letter published by Renier in
Nozze Cian-Sappa-Flandinet, 1894, pp. 244–6, and referred to
hereafter as "Silvestri").

bardment the Spanish artillery caused quite as much damage as that of the French[1]. It fired directly into the massed infantry of the French centre[2], inflicted casualties estimated by an onlooker at 2000[3], and produced a panic among the Gascons[4]. The Spanish infantry, on the other hand, were withdrawn by Pedro Navarro to the low-lying ground close under the embankment of the river[5]. There they lay prone and escaped the effects of the French gunfire[6]. The Spanish cavalry, however, unable to take shelter in this manner, were exposed to the full terrors of the French bombardment, and so intense did it become that they were forced at last by the motive of self-preservation to advance against the enemy.

The exceptional deadliness of the French gunfire was due to the fact that the French gunners succeeded in enfilading the Spanish camp from both flanks. At the crossing of the Ronco some of the French leaders had noticed that the men-at-arms of Fabrizio Colonna's vanguard offered a promising target to guns which should be skilfully placed on the left bank of the river. Two guns, therefore, which had already passed to the right bank, were brought back across the river under the supervision of Alègre

[1] Colonna.
[2] Floranges; Loyal Serviteur; Coccinius; Guicciardini; Giovio, *Vita Alfonsi Ducis Ferrariae* (hereafter referred to as "Giovio, *Ferr.*").
[3] Loyal Serviteur.   [4] Coccinius.
[5] *Relacion* ("ansimesmo de la parte donde estaba nuestro campo, y junto di éste camino estaba nuestra infantería por estar más guardada de el artillería de los franceses"); Guicciardini.
[6] Guicciardini; Loyal Serviteur; Peter Martyr.

and Bayard, and so posted that they fired directly into Colonna's cavalry[1]. This fire on the left flank of the Spaniards was vigorously maintained throughout the period which preceded the hand-to-hand fighting. Still more important was the bombardment developed on the Spanish right. This was the work of the duke of Ferrara[2]. Instead of sending his own guns[3] to co-operate with the French guns in front of the vanguard this famous artillerist took them across the Ronco at a point further downstream from the general crossing-place and then, by a long circuit to the east, brought them at great speed to a spot on the extreme left tip of the curved French line, and therefore to the right flank, and even somewhat to the right rear, of the Spanish encampment. From this spot he wrought great execution among the men-at-arms of the Spanish rearguard[4], and the success with which he was able to enfilade the entire Spanish position is indicated by the fact that he even caused casualties to his own side[5]. He fired furiously and rapidly, and, in conjunction with the guns beyond the Ronco, succeeded in forcing the hands of the Spanish commanders.

The cavalry fight[6].

The result of the heavy losses among the Spanish men-at-arms was that the Spanish cavalry evacuated

---

[1] See Note E, p. 208.   [2] See Note F, p. 209.
[3] 12 heavy guns and 12 light pieces (Guicciardini).
[4] *Relacion*.
[5] Giovio, *Ferr.*; Arluno, *De bello veneto*, bk. IV.
[6] See Note G, p. 211.

the camp and attacked the enemy. The bringing of
the Spanish army to battle had been the aim of
Gaston de Foix from the beginning of the action—
indeed it had been his aim since the beginning of the
campaign—and consequently this first phase of the
engagement marked a distinct tactical success for
the French. The first body of cavalry to go forward
was the rearguard under Carvajal[1]. Padula followed
with the "battle" and Pescara with the light horse.
Carvajal's advance seems to have been a disorderly
one, dictated by panic, and undertaken perhaps
without the viceroy's permission[2]. Padula and Pescara, on the other hand, acted on instructions from
the viceroy and adopted a considered plan of attack.
Pescara undertook to charge the enemy's left flank
while Padula assailed him frontally. The objective
of this double attack was the French "battle." We
may assume therefore that the French "battle" was
no longer behind the general French alignment—or
at any rate that it was no longer screened by other
troops. It seems probable that it had moved to a
position nearer the French centre—a position which
(as we shall see later) had been recently evacuated by
the French infantry[3].

Neither the charge of Carvajal nor the joint attack
of Padula and Pescara was able to break the massed

[1] *Relacion: Historia de le guerre de la beatitudine de Papa
Julio secondo...e del fatto d' arme e saccomano de Ravena,*
Bologna, 1532 (referred to hereafter as *Historia*).

[2] *Relacion* seems to regard Carvajal's advance as spon-
taneous.

[3] At any rate it was separated from the vanguard by grands
fossés according to Bayard.

lances of the French "battle." For this there were several reasons. In the first place, the moral of the Spaniards had been already considerably shaken by the murderous bombardment to which they had been subjected. Then again the route chosen for the main attack was fatal to its orderly accomplishment. Both Carvajal and Padula charged straight forward across a stretch of country much broken by ditches and vegetation, with the result that their formation was destroyed before they reached the enemy. Padula was able to muster only one-third of his men for the vital shock[1]. The chief reason, however, for the ill-success of the Spanish mounted troops was the superior cavalry tactics of the French. Although the strength of the French "battle" was considerably below that of the combined forces of Padula and Pescara it was able, under the direction of Foix, to sustain both the direct and the flank charges by dividing into two bodies and advancing to receive each as a frontal attack[2]. Moreover Palisse, who was left in sole command of the French vanguard (since the duke of Ferrara was engaged on the extreme left with his guns), sent a part of his cavalry to the support of the French "battle[3]" and at the same time summoned Alègre and his reserve from the river crossing[4].

Meanwhile Fabrizio Colonna with the men-at-arms of the Spanish vanguard was still in the camp exposed to the deadly enfilade fire of the French guns.

---

[1] Giovio, *Leo X*; see also Giovio, *Vita Marchionis Piscariae*, bk. I (referred to hereafter as "Giovio, *Pisc.*").

[2] Bayard; Loyal Serviteur; Giovio, *Pisc.*

[3] Colonna.   [4] Pandolfini.

When he saw the disorder of the Spanish cavalry attack and the successful reaction of the French he suggested to Navarro that the time was now ripe for a general advance. Navarro, who had opposed the decision to launch the cavalry, refused to move[1]. Colonna therefore, on his own responsibility, issued from the gap in the defences in front of his position and swept down on the French vanguard, with the intention of preventing further succour being sent to the French "battle[2]." While the two vanguards were thus engaged on the right of the French line, Alègre, previously summoned by Palisse, came galloping along the river-embankment with his 400 lances and followed by the reserve of infantry. He at once fell upon the flank and rear of Fabrizio's force[3]. This arrival of the reserve was the turning point in the cavalry fight. Fabrizio's men-at-arms, attacked in front, in flank, and in rear, began to fly. Some left the field altogether, retreating towards the south and south-west. Others rode across to where Padula and Pescara were sustaining a losing fight against the French "battle[4]." Fabrizio soon found that his command had all but disappeared[5].

[1] Colonna.

[2] *Ibid.*; Pandolfini; Porto. Only Pandolfini (and Nardi, following him) says that it was the French vanguard which Colonna attacked, but Bayard says that the vanguard could not help the "battle" because it "avait affaire ailleurs," thus referring apparently to Colonna's attack on it.

[3] Pandolfini; Guicciardini; Coccinius. Fino and Castello also probably refer to this when they say that the Spanish cavalry was put to flight by French cavalry and infantry.

[4] Coccinius.　　　　　　[5] Colonna.

Alègre, having saved the French vanguard, now advanced to the help of the French "battle." There the fight was more stubborn. For half-an-hour all that survived of the Spanish cavalry supported a bitter hand-to-hand struggle with the bulk of the French gendarmerie[1]. Palisse alone, with what remained to him of the vanguard, held clear from the general engagement. At last Alègre, doubting the issue, sent to Palisse for further assistance, and, in answer to his urgent request, 200 lances[2] and 200 mounted archers and axemen[3] arrived from the French vanguard[4]. These troops extended and enveloped from behind the forces of Padula and Pescara[5]. Both those leaders were taken prisoner and few of their followers escaped. Carvajal and a large proportion of the rearguard succeeded in getting away along the Cesena road[6]. The viceroy, who had not left the camp, joined them in flight. A part of the French men-at-arms[7] and most of the light cavalry[8] took up the pursuit, and the remainder of the French cavalry was left free to play a decisive part in the battle which was now raging between the opposing infantries.

The infantry fight.

Pedro Navarro, true to his tactical principles, did not join battle with his infantry until the enemy tried

---

[1] Loyal Serviteur.
[2] Commanded by the vicomte d'Estoges.
[3] Commanded by the seigneur de Crussol.
[4] Floranges; Loyal Serviteur.　　　[5] Giovio, *Pisc.*
[6] Colonna; Guicciardini.　　　[7] Loyal Serviteur.
[8] Pandolfini.

to force an entrance into his fortified position. When Fabrizio Colonna's men-at-arms advanced to support the remainder of the Spanish cavalry, Navarro's infantry, still lying close to the embankment, were left in sole occupation of the camp[1]. The French command, having by its gunnery successfully drawn the Spanish horse into the open, now turned to the more formidable task of bringing to action the Spanish foot. With this object a double assault was launched against the camp. The French infantry of Molart and the Italian infantry of Bozzolo were withdrawn from the centre and brought across to the river embankment behind the French right. 2000 Gascon crossbowmen and 1000 Picard pikemen were chosen from these and led over the embankment and down on to the narrow strip of land which separated the embankment from the water's edge. Screened by the embankment these troops worked their way along the river's brink towards the enemy's camp, and, when within bowshot range, discharged their arrows over the embankment on to the prone forms of the Spanish infantry[2]. Simultaneously with this diversion at the side of the camp the German infantry moved forward and began to cross the trench which protected the Spanish front[3].

It was now that Navarro took action. The Papal contingent of 2000 Italian infantry which he had under his command was sent out on to the river bank to engage the Gascons[4]. The two leading bodies of

---

[1] *Relacion.*   [2] Loyal Serviteur; *Relacion.*
[3] Coccinius.   [4] Guicciardini; Giovio, *Leo X*.

Spanish foot rose and moved forward to meet the landsknechts[1].

The fight on the river bank was for a time very stubborn. Then the Papal infantry began to waver, probably as a result of the reinforcement of their opponents by fresh French and Italian infantry[2]. Seeing this, two companies of the rear division of the Spanish infantry issued from the camp and joined the fight. At the onset of these highly trained troops the Gascons broke and fled[3]. Molart was killed, and the Spaniards pursued vigorously along the embankment and on each side of it till they reached the French guns[4]. They were pushing yet further forward when they were held up and forced to retrace their steps by a band of French light cavalry[5]. That this defeat of the Gascons took place after the final rout of the Spanish cavalry is proved by the fact that Alègre was free to hurry to the aid of the fugitives and to meet a soldier's death in his efforts to rally them[6].

In the meantime the main force of the Spanish infantry, posted well behind their trench and protected by their armed carts, awaited the onslaught

---

[1] Guicciardini, who, however, does not distinguish here between the different bodies of Spanish foot.

[2] Porto says that the Italian infantry of each side met in combat.

[3] Floranges; Loyal Serviteur; Pandolfini; Guicciardini; Peter Martyr.

[4] *Relacion*; Peter Martyr.

[5] Loyal Serviteur. The Bastard du Fay, Bayard's guidon, was in command of this band.

[6] Loyal Serviteur; Guicciardini; Giovio, *Leo X*.

of the Germans. They allowed a large part of the Germans to cross the trench before they opened fire with their arquebuses[1]. Despite heavy losses the landsknechts pressed on, forced their way through the spears and scythes of the carts and the crossed pikes of their defenders, and engaged in fierce hand-to-hand fighting[2]. It was now that the Spanish swordsmen showed their true tactical worth. Covering themselves with their bucklers they dived under the opposing pikes and cut their way forward among the unprotected legs and thighs of the enemy[3]. With terrible carnage they arrived almost at the centre of the German formation and gave such promise of ultimately disintegrating it that Fabrizio Colonna, who had recently returned almost unaccompanied from the reverse of the Spanish cavalry, began to entertain hopes of snatching victory from defeat[4]. Mustering such few cavalry as he could find he charged and broke that part of the German infantry which had not yet crossed the trench, and then dispersed some Gascons who were reassembling after their defeat by the river[5]. Some of these Gascons fled to those Germans who were engaged with the Spaniards and began to spread panic among them. Landsknechts began to desert the fight and to recross the trench[6]. Fabrizio wrote subsequently that with 200 lances he could have retrieved the fortune of the day. But he

---

[1] Coccinius.   [2] Loyal Serviteur.

[3] Guicciardini; Giovio, *Leo X*; Nardi attributes this tactical method to Pedro Navarro and adds that the swordsmen were specially selected for bodily agility.

[4] Colonna.   [5] *Ibid.*; Coccinius.   [6] Coccinius.

was practically single-handed, and the surviving Italian infantry refused to answer his call to rejoin the fight[1].

The retreat of the Spanish infantry.

At this critical moment the French captains made a supreme effort and consummated the victory. All the cavalry which remained at their disposal was rushed to the scene of the infantry engagement and hurled on the Spaniards from every direction[2]. Foix himself hurried forward and rallied those Germans and Gascons whom Fabrizio's recent charge had dispersed. These footsoldiers now recrossed the trench and joined their comrades in the fight[3], while Foix, hearing now for the first time of the defeat of the Gascons, galloped across to the river bank in the hope of putting a term to the Spanish success in that quarter[4]. The duke of Ferrara left his guns, which had contributed so much to the final victory, collected a troop of men-at-arms, and joined the general assault on the Spanish foot[5]. Other French men-at-arms pushed their way along the embankment to a point well behind the Spanish front, jumped the skirting ditch, charged into the camp, and assaulted the enemy in the rear[6]. The Spaniards, beset on all sides, broke off the fight and attempted to retreat along the river bank. Some two or three thousand

---

[1] Colonna.

[2] Colonna; Jacopo Guicciardini; Guicciardini; Porto; Giovio, *Leo X*; Coccinius; Peter Martyr.   [3] Coccinius.

[4] Loyal Serviteur; Floranges.

[5] Giovio, *Ferr.*; Giovio, *Leo X*.   [6] Floranges.

succeeded in reaching it and marched away unbroken in the direction of Forlì. Fabrizio Colonna was wounded while attempting to protect the rear of the retirement and fell into the hands of the duke of Ferrara. Pedro Navarro, who had no desire to survive the catastrophe, fought on fiercely till he also was disabled and captured.

Meanwhile the youthful commander who had inspired his men with the heroism which exacts victory had fallen in the hour of his triumph. Riding back along the embankment with a handful of men-at-arms in the hope of rallying the Gascons, he found his path barred by the two companies of Spanish infantry who were returning from their successful pursuit of the enemy. No situation could have been more unpropitious for a cavalry charge against massed infantry. The opposing forces were on a narrow causeway with the river on one side and a deep ditch on the other. Foix nevertheless charged the pikes which were levelled against him. He was quickly unhorsed and pierced with many fatal wounds. His fourteen or fifteen followers were likewise put out of action. The Spaniards then pursued their way unopposed and swelled the numbers of those who escaped unbroken from the field[1].

REMARKS.

The duration of the battle. The French started to cross the Ronco as soon as it was light[2], say between 5.30 and 6 a.m. It was not till between 8 a.m. and

---

[1] See Note H, p. 214.   [2] Guicciardini.

9 a.m. that the armies had reached their battle positions and the opening cannonade had begun in earnest[1]. Since this cannonade lasted between two and three hours the cavalry fight must have opened by 11 a.m. By 1 p.m. the Spanish cavalry was probably driven from the field. Between 2 and 3 p.m. the Spanish infantry began to retire[2]. Thus a period of between five and six hours elapsed between the opening of the bombardment and the final defeat of the army of the League[3]. The French men-at-arms who undertook the pursuit of the Spanish cavalry returned to the scene of the battle at 4 p.m., and on the way back by the embankment some of them passed through the retiring Spanish infantry[4].

Casualties. Guicciardini remarks that there is nothing more difficult to decide than the casualties incurred in this battle. Both sides admit the severity of their losses[5]. Silvestri, who visited the battlefield a few days after the fight, was astonished at the number of bodies he found there. He estimated the number at 20,000, but those with experience of

[1] Loyal Serviteur says the battle opened at 8 a.m.: *Relacion* says the French crossing was completed between 8 and 9 a.m.

[2] Jacopo Guicciardini says that the hand-to-hand fighting lasted about four hours, and that the Spanish cavalry was defeated in the first two hours.

[3] Çurita (*Historia del Rey Don Hernando el Catholico*, bk. IX, pp. 282 *seq.*) calls it a five hours battle: Bembo (*Istoria Viniziana*, bk. XII), Mocenico (*Belli cameracensis historiae*, bk. IV), and Reisner (*Historia und Beschreibung Herrn Georgen von Frundsberg*, bk. I, p. 13) a six hours battle.

[4] Loyal Serviteur.

[5] Palisse emphasizes the severity of the French losses in his letter to Louis XII (quoted in Chabannes, *Preuves pour servir à l'histoire de la maison de Chabannes*, vol. I, p. 433).

stricken fields will, in the case of casualty estimates, be inclined to reject the statements of eyewitnesses in favour of those based on calculation. Only one writer, the German Kochlin or Coccinius, claims to have based his calculation of the casualties on careful investigation. He estimates the casualties on the French side at 3000 and those on the side of the League at 9000. As to his estimate of the French losses, Guicciardini and the Loyal Serviteur are roughly in agreement with it. On the question of the Spanish losses there is less agreement. The Portuguese report[1] and Venetian writers[2] make the losses on each side about equal. Guicciardini estimates the Spanish losses at twice those of the French. The Loyal Serviteur and Silvestri agree with Coccinius in estimating the Spanish casualties at three times those of the French. Now it should be noted that Silvestri, the visitor to the battlefield, is a much more credible witness when he estimates the ratio between the Spanish and the French dead than when he merely gives his idea of the total numbers. When he says that he saw 20,000 bodies he is simply guessing: when he says that for every corpse belonging to the French side he saw three corpses belonging to the Spanish and Papal side, he is making a calculation which is not beyond the powers of a casual observer. Consequently the fact that his ratio agrees with the ratio given by Coccinius—the only writer who based his calculation on careful investigation—provides

[1] In *Corp. dipl. Portug.* vol. I, p. 164.
[2] *E.g.* Bembo (*loc. cit.*) and Mocenico (*loc. cit.*).

us with a strong reason for accepting the figures of the painstaking German, which are in detail: 9000 slain among the soldiers of the Holy League, 1000 among the landsknechts, and 2000 among the other troops of the French army.

It should be noted that at the time of the battle of Ravenna the slain were the only casualties, with the exception of distinguished prisoners, in which the historian took an interest. The modern tabulation of minor casualties was not indulged in.

Causes of the French victory. The battle of Ravenna was the triumph of co-ordinated action over unco-ordinated action. The root cause of the French success was the weakness of Spanish and Papal command. The Spanish and Papal army was under the supreme direction of a man who was unversed in the art of war. Although the viceroy was supported by several professional captains, his inability to weigh and compare the advice they gave him turned what should have been a source of strength into a weakness. When battle was once joined the Spanish army became the sport of divided command. The viceroy sent the cavalry of the rearguard and "battle" into the fight without first apprising Fabrizio Colonna of his intention. Fabrizio led the vanguard into action without waiting for orders or notifying his superior commander. Pedro Navarro played an independent rôle throughout the day. It was due to his influence that the Spanish army stood at first on the defensive. When the viceroy changed his plans and attacked the enemy, Navarro still adhered, as far as his own command was concerned, to his original tactical conception. The consequence was that the Spanish cavalry fled before the infantry came into action, and the subsequent heroism of the infantry was quite unable to retrieve the initial disaster.

In marked contrast to this confusion and waste of effort is the happy correlation of the French methods. Although there was on the French side nothing corresponding to modern staff work, the general supervision exercised by Foix and the willingness with which each section co-operated with the others for the common end, infused into their tactics a coherence which a prearranged plan could hardly have achieved. The secret of this unity of action lay in the personality of the young French commander. Gaston de Foix had already inspired his men to undertake with success the most formidable military enterprises, he had erased the word impossible from his dictionary and had at the same time engendered in their minds a blind confidence in his leadership. Soldiers so led will not readily admit defeat. They acquire moreover a corporate tradition which tends almost unconsciously to unify their actions on the field of battle. Hence at Ravenna the French possessed a moral advantage over adversaries commanded by a civil administrator who was a prey to the hesitancy and the panic which the clash of arms is apt to produce in the inexperienced. The crisis in the Spanish effort occurred when the Spanish cavalry was defeated: it was this moment which the viceroy chose to beat his precipitate retreat. The crisis in the French effort occurred when the Gascons broke and the Germans wavered: it was then that Foix set all his forces in motion for a supreme concerted attack. In this way the battle of Ravenna illustrates how warfare, which is at bottom a conflict of wills, depends for its decisions on human personality.

NOTES

Note A.

For the topography of the battlefield I have, in addition to the contemporary authorities, made use of:

(*a*) "Mappa fatta per mostrare la Linea della nuova navigazione," etc. (Andrea Bolzoni Ferrarese Intagliò l' Anno 1739).

(*b*) "Battaglia e saccheggio di Ravenna avvenuti l' anno 1512. Breve relazione scritta da Don Sante Ghigi sacerdote ravennate nell' annc 1905" (Bagnacavallo, Scuola tip. del Ricreatorio 1906).

From the Mappa I learned the ancient courses of the Ronco and Montone, and from it I adapted my own map. With regard to all other topographical details I have followed closely Don Sante Ghigi's monograph. *E.g.*, from him I learn:

(*a*) the position of Foix's two bridges (pp. 51–2, 85);

(*b*) the fact that the argini were then lower than they are now (p. 75) and served as roads between Ravenna and Forlì (p. 59);

(*c*) the site of the Spanish encampment (p. 75).

On two further points which perplex me I should have welcomed an opinion from Don Sante Ghigi, viz.:

(*a*) the actual height of the argini in 1512;

(*b*) the width of the strip of land between the argine and the river in early April after a very snowy winter (as that of 1511–12 was).

As to the height of the argine, the historians of the battle make it quite obvious that, despite its flanking ditch, infantry and cavalry could mount it with comparative ease.

On the width of the river bank depends the question of the exact position of the gap in the Spanish trench. Pandolfini, whose description of it is copied by the Florentine historians (*e.g.* Guicciardini, Nardi), says: "nella fronte, tra il fiume e il principio del fosso, avevano lassato circa a 20 braccia di spazio, per potere avere esito ad assaltare gli nemici tra il fiume e il fosso," which seems to show that the gap included, if it did not coincide with, the space between the river and the argine. But it is worth noticing that Pandolfini does not mention the argine, though he speaks elsewhere of the "riva" and of the "via del fiume" and of the "ripe" which were levelled for the French crossing. My view is that the 20 braccia space was all on that side of the argine which was further from the river and that the Spaniards regarded the argine as the left-hand boundary of their camp.

In this connexion I differ in one small point from Don Sante Ghigi. He thinks it was to the space between the argine and the river that Navarro withdrew his infantry in order to escape the artillery fire. This would certainly seem to have been the best refuge from guns firing from the right flank (as the duke of Ferrara's were), but it should be remarked: (*a*) that such a position, while perhaps giving more shelter from the duke of Ferrara's guns, would have exposed the infantry more to the gunfire from the further bank of the river; (*b*) that no historian actually says that the infantry lay in that spot: the historians use indefinite phrases such as "in luogo basso a canto all' argine" (Guicciardini), or "de la parte donde estaba nuestro campo, y junto de éste camino" (the writer of the *Relacion*); yet each of these writers can in other connexions refer explicitly to the lower ground by the water's edge.

Note B.

For the numbers of each army I have followed the document in Sanuto (*Diarii*, XIV, pp. 170–4). This is apparently a copy of the official paper strength of the two armies. *E.g.* it gives the number of the Spanish infantry as 9000 and that of the Papal infantry as 2000: the writer of the *Relacion*, on the other hand, says that, while the figures 9000 and 2000 represent the numbers on the pay rolls, the actual numbers taking part in the battle were not above 7000 and 1500 respectively. In the same way the other numbers given in the text are no doubt in excess of the actual fighting strength of the different units, but, provided this is realized, they give a better idea of the actual and relative numbers of both sides than can be drawn from the very conflicting testimony of historians.

Note C.

As to the relative positions of the cavalry of the French vanguard and that of the French "battle," Guicciardini distinctly says that the cavalry of the "battle" were in rear of the front line, while Pandolfini, with whose account he was acquainted and with whom he generally agrees, says that they were near the cavalry of the vanguard and in line with the infantry (the infantry being a part of the front line). Guicciardini does not contradict Pandolfini by saying that the cavalry of the "battle" were behind the cavalry of the vanguard. The only conflict is as to which of these two bodies was out of the general alignment. Guicciardini's statement that the cavalry of the "battle" were in reserve points to the conclusion that it was they who were in rear of the front line.

Note D.

The passage in Porto (*Lettere Storiche*, no. 66) describing these carts is as follows:

[Pedro Navarro] prese certe carrette a due ruote, fatte di legname leggiero, con un tiemo lungo d' intorno sei piedi, aveva posti nella lor fronte alcuni spiedi di ferro, lunghi quasi una lancia di cavallo, acutissimi, e annodati ad alcuni archibugi gagliardi, già inchiodati presso di loro sopra le dette carrette. Le quali, collocate nella spianata tutto intorno de' fanti, erano di tanta agevolezza, che da essi fanti potevano essere spinte o ritirate facilmente. Cinti adunque da quelle, potevano i fanti camminare per la piana campagna, e dove loro piacesse fermarsi, pontando i detti tiemi a terra, e mercè gli spiedi stando securi dal furiosissimo urto delle gente d' arme di Francia, la cui vigoria solamente temevano. Potevano similmente, tirando gli archibusi a' nemici, uscire delle carrette, e a tempo e luogo ricoverandovisi fare loro gravissimo danno.

Coccinius says:

Habebant ante se currus quam plurimos, in quibus collocaverant bombardas quas arcusbusos Itali vocant, Germani vero hackbuchsen; eisdem praeterea curribus infixerant instrumentum cum tribus acutissimis ferris, duo eius ferramenta, quae dextra et sinistra respiciebant, erant curva instar falcium, id, vero quod in ante prospiciebat erat prolongum et rectum, et dein supra id instrumentum currui infixum disposuerant lanceas oblique locatas.

Note E.

The Loyal Serviteur particularly mentions these two guns—a cannon and a long culverin. They were mounted near the river crossing, probably under the supervision of Alègre. According to the Loyal Serviteur it was these guns which caused the chief loss to Fabrizio Colonna's men-at-arms. In support of his account we may cite:

(1) Fino, who says that the French artillery fired "di l' una et l' altra banda";

(2) Carondelet, who says that the French artillery was placed "de trois coustés fort à leur avantage";

(3) Floranges, who mentions French guns which bombarded the Spanish men-at-arms who were "de là de l'eau";

(4) Çurita, who says "mas la [artilleria] de los enemigos, despues que se puso en orden, por ser doblada que

la del campo de la liga, y assentarse en lo otra ribera del rio, en lugar mas abierto, y tendido, sobre la parte de nuestro campo, por el lado, y frente del, hizo grandissimo danno en toda la gente de armas, que no tenia ningun reparo."

Note F.

Most contemporary historians say that guns were moved from the French front to the French left flank. Two writers (not historians) who were present, viz. Pandolfini and Castello make this statement, but it is significant that those two writers do not say that it was the duke of Ferrara who was responsible for the move. Pandolfini says that Foix

> fece levar l' armata dell' artiglierie che era nella fronte alle gente d' arme e condurle nella punta dell' esercito suo in su la sinistra dove erano gli arcieri.

Castello says that the French

> loco voltorono le artiglierie grosse tutte a l' incontro per faccia di li Spagnoli e le mezano al fianco de la bataglia spagnola.

Yet it is certain that it was the duke of Ferrara who was responsible for bringing guns on to the Spanish right: contemporary historians are unanimous on the point. Most of them (e.g. Guicciardini) are content to apply Pandolfini's statement to the duke of Ferrara.

But Giovio, who was a personal friend of the duke of Ferrara, says nothing about the duke's guns coming first into action on the French front. He implies that the duke manoeuvred his guns independently from the beginning (Porto also implies this), and he is the only writer who makes mention of the route taken by the duke. His words are

> tormenta unius praecipue Alfonsi consilio amnem, loco mare versus a castris hostium inferiore, sunt traducta, quae mox ille ita magno in obliquum cir-

cuitu provexit, ut a latus et terga hostium citatis
iumentis verterentur (*Vita Leonis X*, bk. 11);

and again

Alfonsus re multum ante provisa, atque opportune
administrata, lato versus mare flexu capto, pecu-
liaria sua tormenta edoctis aurigis et libratoribus,
in terga lateraque hostium direxerat (*Vita Alfonsi
Ducis Ferrariae*).

Now a number of heavy guns cannot be moved about
at will over land cut up with ditches (cf. Peter Martyr's
description of the battlefield: "sunt fossae manu factae
quae superfluas pluviarum tempore inducant aquas ad
fluvios"). The duke of Ferrara had to discover a road
by which he could get his guns to the Spanish right flank.
There were only two likely roads, viz. those marked
AAA and *BBB* on Map III. If he came into action first
on the French right and then decided to work round to
the French left he would have, in order to get to either of
these roads, to go back almost to Ravenna, and he would
not have finished the manoeuvre as soon as we know that
he did. Hence I think that he did not come into action
on the French right at all, but that he manoeuvred his
guns independently from the beginning.

The route *AAA* may have been barred by hostile light
cavalry: at any rate it passed dangerously near the
Spanish position: nor does it answer to Giovio's phrases
"magno in obliquum circuitu" and "lato versus mare
flexu capto." Both these phrases fit the route *BBB*, and
it is my opinion that the duke came by that route to the
neighbourhood of point *X*, whence he could bring lateral
fire to bear on the Spanish army and especially on the
Spanish rearguard (as we know from the writer of the
Relacion that he did). For this journey, which is roughly
six English miles, he would require, say, an hour. If he
started when the French army crossed the Ronco, then
his guns would have come into action, at the latest,
about half-way through the preliminary bombardment.

Note G.

The cavalry action is the most difficult part of the battle of Ravenna to unravel from the accounts of the authorities.

(1) As to the order in which the different bodies of Spanish cavalry advanced, I have followed Fabrizio Colonna and the writer of the *Relacion*, who are certainly the best authorities. Porto and Castello support them.

(2) It is more difficult to decide which bodies of cavalry fought against which. To begin with we may dismiss as a blunder Guicciardini's statement that Palisse was in command of the French "battle," since Pandolfini, the Loyal Serviteur, Floranges, and the authority quoted in Sanuto XIV, pp. 170–4, unite in putting him with the duke of Ferrara in command of the vanguard. Since the duke of Ferrara was absent with his guns, Palisse therefore remained in sole command of the vanguard.

(3) Bayard, Pandolfini, and Vignati say that the opening attack (*i.e.* that of the Spanish rearguard, "battle," and light cavalry) was directed against the French "battle." The Loyal Serviteur, on the other hand, says that the French "battle" was attacked by Fabrizio Colonna. Now the Loyal Serviteur, in saying this, is quite plainly referring to the opening attack (and we know from Fabrizio Colonna and from the *Relacion* that Fabrizio's was not the opening attack), and he describes it as a converging attack of two troops (which that of Padula and Pescara was). We know further that the body of men-at-arms and light cavalry which eventually came and enveloped Padula and Pescara (see Giovio's *Vita Marchionis Piscariae*, bk. 1) was sent by Palisse from the French vanguard (see the accounts of the Loyal Serviteur and of Floranges). We may therefore conclude that it was not Palisse's force (*i.e.* the vanguard) but the "battle" against which Carvajal, Padula, and Pescara led their men.

(4) Fabrizio Colonna says that he advanced in support of Carvajal, Padula, and Pescara because he saw they

were in difficulties, having a part of the French vanguard against them. If we assume that this means that a part of the French vanguard was detached by Palisse to help the French "battle," then the different descriptions of subsequent events tally fairly well.

(5) Pandolfini says that Fabrizio, when he advanced, attacked the French vanguard, which must mean of course that part of the French vanguard which had not gone to the help of the "battle." At this stage therefore we have Padula and Pescara and Carvajal engaged in a losing fight with the French "battle" and a part of the French vanguard, and Fabrizio Colonna engaged with the remainder of the French vanguard commanded by Palisse.

(6) When Alègre arrived with the reserve he certainly attacked Fabrizio Colonna first, as witness Pandolfini, Fino, Castello, Coccinius, and Guicciardini. Coccinius tells us that some of the routed Spanish vanguard fled to the Spanish rearguard, which was engaged with the French "battle." We must assume that Alègre followed them, since both Floranges and the Loyal Serviteur represent him later as sending for help to Palisse, while Giovio (*Vita Marchionis Piscariae*) and Coccinius agree with Floranges and the Loyal Serviteur that it was this final help from Palisse which decided the cavalry engagement and led to the capture of Padula and Pescara.

It is interesting to note that the actions of Palisse are the deciding factor throughout this phase of the battle. His early reinforcements helped the French "battle" to withstand the first onset of the Spanish cavalry, his summoning of Alègre led to the rout of the Spanish vanguard, and his second reinforcement of the French "battle" finally turned the scale.

The course of the cavalry engagement as set out in the text may be put shortly as follows, with the authorities for each statement bracketed after it:

The first Spanish cavalry to engage, attack the French "battle" (Bayard, Serviteur, Vignati): this Spanish cavalry was that of (a) Carvajal, followed by that of

(b) Padula and Pescara (*Relacion*, Fabrizio Colonna, Castello, *Historia*).

This Spanish cavalry makes two converging attacks and a part of the French "battle" receives each attack frontally (Serviteur, Giovio, *Pisc.*).

Palisse, in command of French vanguard (Floranges, Serviteur, Pandolfini, Sanuto XIV, 170–4), sends a part of the French vanguard to help the French "battle" (Fabrizio Colonna).

He also summons Alègre (Pandolfini).

Fabrizio Colonna, seeing the Spanish cavalry of the "battle" and rearguard hard pressed, advances with the Spanish vanguard to support them (Fabrizio Colonna, Porto, and, apparently, Floranges) and attacks the French vanguard (Pandolfini).

Alègre arrives from the river-road (Pandolfini) and attacks Fabrizio Colonna in flank with cavalry and infantry (Pandolfini, Fino, Coccinius, Guicciardini).

Fabrizio's men break and fly, some from the field (Fino, Castello), some to their rearguard (Coccinius).

Alègre follows the latter (inference from the events which follow) and fights in support of the French "battle" for half an hour (Serviteur).

He then sends (Serviteur) or goes (Floranges) for help to Palisse, who sends (Floranges, Serviteur) men-at-arms and mounted archers (Floranges, Serviteur, Giovio, *Pisc.*).

This reinforcement causes the final rout of the Spanish cavalry (Floranges, Serviteur, Giovio, *Pisc.*, Coccinius) and Pescara is taken prisoner (Floranges, Giovio, *Pisc.*).

The Spanish vanguard had been practically annihilated (Fabrizio Colonna, *Relacion*, Jacopo Guicciardini, Porto).

The viceroy gets away with the remains of the rearguard (Guicciardini, Giovio, *Leo X*).

N.B. (a) It is significant that Fabrizio Colonna has little to say about his own fighting: it has to be pieced together from the remarks of others. We are therefore probably right in attributing to his command a very modest part in the actual engagement.

(b) Little is said by any writer about the exploits of the men-at-arms of the Spanish rearguard. Fabrizio Colonna, the *Relacion*, Castello, Guicciardini and the *Historia* vouch for their opening the fight. Giovio: *Vita Leonis X* and Guicciardini tell us that they escaped with little loss. They were apparently the first to fly—and the viceroy with them. The brunt of the cavalry fight seems to have been borne by the "battle."

Note H.

Some writers (*e.g.* Pandolfini, Fino, Vignati, Grumello, Anshelm) state that Foix was killed rallying the French infantry. Others that he was killed charging the Spanish infantry as they retired. The conflict between these two versions is considerably lessened if we accept the statement of the Loyal Serviteur and of Floranges that it was the news of the defeat of the Gascons which prompted him to ride across to the scene of that disaster, namely, to the river-road. On the river-road, according to the Loyal Serviteur, he met and charged, with fatal results to himself, the two Spanish companies which were returning from the pursuit of the Gascons. Most writers who heard (correctly, as I think) that Foix was killed while charging the retiring Spanish infantry naturally assumed that the infantry in question was the main body (*i.e.* the vanguard and "battle") which had been engaged with the landsknechts. I am led to accept the Loyal Serviteur's statement that the fatal charge was made against the troops of the Spanish rearguard returning from the pursuit of the Gascons by

(a) its reasonableness as an explanation of the tragedy;

(b) its particularity, pointing to first-hand information; Cf. "[Foix] se va gecter sur ceste chaussée par laquelle se retiroient ses deux enseignes qui le vont rencontrer en leur chemin...la chaussée étoit estroicte, et d'ung costé le canal où on ne povoit descendre; de l'autre y avoit ung merveilleux fossé que l'on ne povoit passer. Brief, tous ceux qui estoient avecques le duc de Nemours furent gectez en l'eaue ou tumbez dedens le fossé" (*Hist. de Bayart*, ch. LIV);

(*c*) the striking support given to it by the account in the *Relacion*, viz.: "y como quiera que Monsieur de Fox... él y los que con él estaban...los cuales estaban en el mesmo camino, viése ansí retraerse á los espanoles, con sus banderas y estandartes enarbolados, arremete él y todos los que con él estaban; y como los nuestros los viesen ir á éllos, con muy esforzado ánimo les reciben y esperan con las picas, y de tal manera los nuestros los embisten, que no quedaron en pié viente de todos los franceses porque como el rio estoviese junto del mesmo camino y fuese tan hondo de ribera, como los nuestros los encontraron, dieron con éllos abajo en lo rio";

(*d*) Grumello's phrase that Foix was killed "pigliato il camino de epsi infanti" may mean that he barred their path;

(*e*) if Foix had been killed in the main fight there would have been less uncertainty about the actual circumstances of his death.

APPENDIX B

LIST OF BOOKS CONSULTED

I. Modern Works.

Oman. Art of War in the Middle Ages.
—— Art of War in the Middle Ages (Lothian Essay).
Jähns. Handbuch einer Geschichte des Kriegswesens.
—— Geschichte des Kriegswissenschaft.
Rüstow. Geschichte der Infanterie.
La Barre Duparcq. L'art de la guerre.
Ricotti. Storia delle compagnie di ventura.
Canestrini. Della milizia italiana.
Ronzani e Luciolli. Le fabbriche civili, ecclesiastiche, e militari di Michele Sanmicheli (ed. Zanotto: Genova, undated). A collection of engravings.
Villari. Machiavelli and his times.

II. General Contemporary Histories.
A. *Italian*.

Guicciardini. Istoria d' Italia.
Giovio (Jovius). Istorie del suo tempo (trans. Domenichi: Venice 1581). Books v–x and xix–xxiv inclusive are of doubtful authenticity.
—— Vita Consalvi Cordubae.
—— Vita Marchionis Piscariae.
—— Vita Leonis X.
—— Vita Alfonsi Ferrariae.
—— Elogia clarorum virorum.
Sanuto. La spedizione di Carlo VIII in Italia.
Priuli. De bello gallico (attributed to Sanuto by Muratori, Rerum Italicarum Scriptores, vol. xxiv).

Rucellai (Oricellarius). De bello italico.
Specianus. De bello gallico.
Vegius. Historia.
—— Ephemerides.
Vettori. Sommario della storia d' Italia 1511–27.
Florus. De bello italico.
Rossi. Vita di Giovanni de' Medici.
Benedetti (Benedictus). Il fatto d' arme del Tarro.

B. *Foreign.*

D'Auton. Chroniques de Louis XII.
Seyssel. L'excellence et la félicité de la victoire que eut
le Très chrestien Roy de France...au lieu appelé
Aignadel.
Champier. Le Triomphe du Thres-chrestien Roy.
—— Les Gestes ensemble la Vie du preulx Chevalier
Bayard.
Loyal Serviteur. Histoire de Bayart.
Marillac. Vie du connétable de Bourbon.
Ferronus. De rebus gestis Gallorum.
Gilles. Les...Annalles des...Moderateurs des belliqueuses
Gaulles.
Coccinius. De bellis italicis.
Nauclerus. Chronicon (with Nicolai Baselii Additio).
Reisner. Historia und Beschreibung Herrn Georgen von
Frundsberg.

III. Local Italian Histories
and Chronicles.

Guicciardini. Istoria Fiorentina.
Nardi. Istorie della città di Firenze.
Varchi. Storia Fiorentina.
Segni. Storie Fiorentine.
Pitti. Istoria Fiorentina.
—— Vita di Antonio Giacomini.
Nerli. Commentarii de' fatti civili occorsi dentro la città
di Firenze 1215–1537.

Bembo. Istoria Viniziana.
Mocenico. La guerra di Cambrai.
Malipiero. Annali Veneti.
Arluno. De bello veneto.
Prato. De rebus mediolanensibus sui temporis.
Cagnola. Storia di Milano.
Burigozzo. Cronica Milanese.
Merula. Chronicon.
Ambrogio da Paullo. Cronaca Milanese.
Muraltus. Annalia.
Senarega. De rebus genuensibus commentaria.
Albino. De bello gallico.
Feltrio. Cronica.
Coniger. Coronache.
Cronica Anonima 1495–1519.
Grumello. Cronaca.
Carpesano. Commentaria suorum temporum.
Cronache Cremonesi 1494–1525.
Sardi. Libro delle Historie Ferraresi.
Joseph ben Joshua ben Meir. Chronicles (trans. C. H. F.
      Bialloblotzky).
Anselmi. Descrittione del sacco di Brescia 1512.
Cordo. La obsidione di Padua (verse).

IV. Diaries.

Sanuto. Diarii.
Buonaccorsi. Diario.
Landucci. Diario Fiorentino.
Passero. Giornali.
Guarino. Diario.
Grassi. Diario di Papa Leone X.
Portoveneri. Memoriale.
Pezzati. Diario della ribellione della città d' Arezzo.
Diario Ferrarese.
Delavigne. Vergier d'honneur.
—— Voyage de Naples.
Troyes. Relation.
Barrillon. Journal.

V. MÉMOIRES.

Commines. Mémoires.
Villeneuve. Mémoires.
Floranges (Fleuranges). Mémoires.
Du Bellay. Mémoires.
Monluc. Mémoires.
Sauli. Autobiografia.
Perizolo. Ricordi.

VI. LETTERS, DISPATCHES, ETC.

Charles VIII. Lettres (ed. Pélicier).
La Pilorgerie. Campagnes et bulletins de Charles VIII.
Maximilian I. Correspondance 1507–19 (ed. Le Glay).
Francis I. Lettre à la duchesse d'Angoulesme sur la
    bataille de Marignan (in Pétitot, Collection, vol.
    XVII, p. 184).
Morone. Documenti che concernono la vita pubblica di
    Girolamo Morone (ed. Müller, Misc. di Stor. It.,
    vol. III).
—— Ricordi Inediti.
Commines. Lettres.
Relazioni of the Venetian Ambassadors.
Machiavelli. Legazioni e commissarie.
Provisione della Milizia e Ordinanza del Popolo Fioren-
    tino 1528.
Giustinian. Dispacci.
V. Vitelli. Lettere.
G. P. Vitelli. Parere sul modo di riavere Pisa 1497.
Giacomini. Lettere scritte alla Signoria di Firenze sull' im-
    presa di Pisa.
Porto. Lettere Storiche.
Sanmicheli. Discorso circa il fortificar la città di Udine.

VII. CONTEMPORARY WORKS ON THE ART OF WAR.

Francesco di Giorgio Martini. Trattato di architettura
    civile e militare.
Philippe duc de Clèves. Instruction de toutes les ma-
    nieres de guerroyer.

Machiavelli. Il Principe.

—— Discorsi sopra la prima deca di Tito Livio.

—— Arte della guerra.

Vallo. Libro continente appertenentie ad capitanii.

Joannes Thomae von Venedig. Ein Discurs...von Be-
    schützung und Eroberung der Vestungen (in
    Zetter, Kriegs und Archeley Kunst, ch. cxiii).

Tartaglia. Quesiti et inventioni diverse.

also:

Flavius Vegetius. De re militari.

VIII. For the Battle of Ravenna.

A. *Accounts by persons who were present.*

Floranges. Mémoires, vol. i, pp. 88 *seq.* (in the edition
    published by the Société de l'histoire de France).

Bayard. Letter of 14 April 1512 (App. III in the edition
    of the Loyal Serviteur published by the Soc. de
    l'hist. de France).

Loyal Serviteur. Histoire de Bayart, ch. liv.

Palisse (Jacques de Chabannes, seigneur de la). Letter of
    11 April 1512 (in Chabannes, Preuves pour servir
    à l'histoire de la maison de Chabannes, vol. i,
    p. 433).

Pandolfini. Letter of 11 April 1512 (in Desjardins, Né-
    gociations diplomatiques de la France avec la
    Toscane, vol. ii, p. 581).

Fino. Letter of 11 April 1512 (in Tommasini, Niccolò
    Machiavelli, vol. i, p. 706).

Carondelet. Letter to Marguerite d'Autriche (in Lettres
    de Louis XII, vol. iii, p. 227).

Vignati. Cronaca (in Arch. Stor. Lomb. 2nd Series, vol. i,
    p. 593).

Castello. Depositione (in Sanuto, Diarii, vol. xiv, col.
    128).

Fabrizio Colonna. Letter of 28 April 1512 (in Sanuto,
    Diarii, vol. xiv, col. 176).

Relacion de los sucesos de las armas de España en Italia
en los años de 1511 y 1512 con la jornada de
Rávena (in Coleccion de documentos ineditos para
la historia de España, vol. LXXIX, p. 274).

B. *Accounts in contemporary letters.*

Porto. Lettere Storiche, no. 66.

Jacopo Guicciardini. Letter of 11 April 1512 (in Arch.
Stor. It., Series I, vol. XV, pp. 307–19).

Silvestri. Letter of 16 April 1512 (in Nozze Cian-Sappa-
Flandinet 1894, p. 244).

Letter from Mantua (in Sanuto, Diarii, vol. XIV, col. 126).

Letter to missier Nicolo (ibid. col. 151).

The Portuguese Report (in Corp. dipl. Portug., vol. I,
p. 164).

Peter Martyr. Opus Epistolarum, no. CCCLXXXIII.

Scheurl. Briefbuch, p. 86.

C. *Local accounts.*

Letter from Bologna (in Sanuto, Diarii, vol. XIV, col. 145).

Depositione of Frate Constantino 23 April 1512 (ibid. col.
154).

Historia de le guerre de la beatitudine de papa Julio
secondo contra el christianiss. Re de Francia…e
del fatto d' arme e saccomano de Ravena. (Poem
published at Bologna 1532.)

El facto d' arme de Romagna: con la presa de Ravenna.
(Poem undated.)

D. *Accounts by well-informed Contemporaries.*

I. *Italian.*

Guicciardini. Istoria d' Italia, bk. X.

Giovio. Vita Marchionis Piscariae, bk. I.

—— Vita Leonis X, bk. II.

—— Vita Alfonsi Ducis Ferrariae.

Buonaccorsi. Diario, p. 170.

Nardi. Istorie della città di Firenze, bk. v.
Bembo. Istoria Viniziana, bk. xii.
Mocenico. Belli cameracensis historiae, bk. iv.
Cf. also the lists of dead, etc., in Sanuto, Diarii, vol. xiv,
coll. 148–51 and the statement of the composition
of the armies in the same volume, coll. 170–4.

2. *Spanish.*

Document No. 23 in Documentos relativos a la historia
del Conde Pedro Navarro (in Coleccion de documentos ineditos, vol. xxvi, p. 5).
Çurita. Historia de Rey Don Hernando el Catholico,
bk. ix, p. 282 (not contemporary but as official
historiographer of Aragon he had access to contemporary documents).

3. *German and Swiss.*

Coccinius. De bellis italicis.
Reisner. Historia und Beschreibung Herrn Georgen von
Frundsberg, bk. i, p. 13.
Zwingli. De gestis inter Gallos et Helveticos ad Raven-
nam (in Schuler and Schulthess's edition of
Zwingli's works, vol. iv, p. 167).
Anshelm. Berner-Chronik, vol. iv, p. 207.

4. *French.*

Ferronus. De rebus gestis Gallorum, bk. iv.

E. *Other contemporary accounts.*

Arluno. De bello veneto, bk. iv.
Prato. De rebus mediolanensibus.
Grumello. Cronaca, cap. xv.
Joseph ben Joshua ben Meir. Chronicles, para. 507 (trans.
C. H. F. Bialloblotzky).
Machiavelli. Discorsi, bk. ii, ch. xvii.

Carpesanus. Commentarii suorum temporum, bk. v, col. 1284.

Sardi. Libro delle Historie Ferraresi, bk. xi.

Muraltus. Annalia, cap. xxix.

Gilles. Les...Annalles des...Moderateurs des belliqueuses Gaulles, Feuillet cxxxv.

Champier. Gestes de Bayard, bk. ii, ch. x.

Bernaldez. Historia de los Reyes Catolicos Don Fernando y Doña Isabel, cap. ccxxxi.

INDEX